# *Called*

## BARBARA CAWTHORNE CRAFTON

Church Publishing
NEW YORK

Unless otherwise noted, the Scripture quotations contained herein are from the New Revised Standard Version Bible, copyright © 1989 by the Division of Christian Education of the National Council of Churches of Christ in the U.S.A. Used by permission. All rights reserved.

Church Publishing, 19 East 34th Street, New York, NY 10016

www.churchpublishing.org

Cover art: Annunciation, original painting by Valerie Dean, courtesy of Francis Iles Gallery Rochester, UK
Cover design by Jennifer Kopec, 2Pug Design
Typeset by Denise Hoff

Library of Congress Cataloging-in-Publication Data

Names: Crafton, Barbara Cawthorne, author.
Title: Called / Barbara Cawthorne Crafton.
Description: New York : Church Publishing, 2017.

Identifiers: LCCN 2016038573 (print) | LCCN 2016045333 (ebook) | ISBN 9780819232915 (pbk.) | ISBN 9780819232922 (ebook)

Subjects: LCSH: Clergy--Appointment, call, and election. | Vocation, Ecclesiastical. | Pastoral theology.
Classification: LCC BV4011.4 .C39 2017 (print) | LCC BV4011.4 (ebook) | DDC 253/.2--dc23
LC record available at https://lccn.loc.gov/2016038573

Printed in the United States of America

*This book is dedicated with affection and respect to*
*Constance Coles and Charles Simmons,*
*Canons for Ministry in the Episcopal Diocese of New York,*
*with memories of many*
*soul-satisfying retreats together,*
*as well as to all the students and ordinands*
*they have shepherded over the years.*

# CONTENTS

## INTRODUCTION

# BEFORE I FORMED YOU IN THE WOMB, I KNEW YOU

**FRIENDS OF MINE WHO WENT TO** Roman Catholic schools remember the priest coming in once or twice every year to talk to the class about vocations. Boys and girls would get separate talks, one of the nuns telling the girls what being a sister was like. These talks were about Vocation, with a capital V. The word was not used about any walk of life other than the priesthood or the convent. "How many vocations have you had from your parish?" one priest will ask another. What he means is, has anybody become a priest? Vocation seen this way is God's calling a person out of a secular occupation into professional religious life.

But how likely is it, really, that the only kind of vocation that would interest God would be one involving church? In a medieval Christian worldview that would make some sense: The creation begins with stars and water and rocks, progressing through plants, animals, and human beings, the overseers of them all. It culminates in the church, whose earthly splendors mirror heavenly ones. But we do not see creation that way now, knowing what we now know about the origins of things, about worlds too numerous for us even to imagine the number of them. The ladder of ascending worth natural to an ancient understanding of the cosmos fits ours less well.

Surely the imagination of God, which has spoken everything into being and continues to do so, encompasses and permeates more than the ecclesial arrangements of our age or any other. My friend Jim compares the church to a scaffold—it is not the building itself, but the contingent structure *surrounding* the building, which makes it possible to construct the building. The building itself is God's relationship with us, a relationship of creation and love so intimate that, in its fulfillment, the scaffold falls away and we are one with God.

I love the church. I have spent a lifetime serving in it, have seen its faults up close, and love it still. But I have never thought that God can only be found and served there, or even that the encounter with God in an ecclesial setting trumps all other encounters with God. If the Incarnation means anything at all, surely it must mean that the whole creation is holy, that every human activity is available to be filled with the Spirit. And surely the radical love that brings us into being does not rank us, one above or below another. Each of us has a unique place in the universe without which, however small a part of it we may be, the universe would not be quite what it is. Everything that exists, exists importantly. Hierarchy is our invention, not God's.

Thus, I am impatient with a narrow view of call that limits it to participation in church structures. Each of us is called to something. The hope for every newborn is that she will grow to adulthood and find the walk of life that uses every ounce of what makes her who she is, that she will spend it all here, leaving nothing behind when she leaves us. I see no reason why there might not be more than one such walk of life, for some people: vocations which have their season and come to an end, to be supplanted by something new.

I also tire easily of notions of call that locate it exclusively outside of our own will. People are forever asking themselves what they are "supposed to do." What they are "supposed to be." Whom they are "supposed to marry." You're not supposed to marry anybody. You *might* marry someone, and if you do I hope that you will use every faculty you have at your disposal in deciding who that someone might be: your rational mind, your knowledge of yourself and of the world in which you live, your understanding of the difference between hope and magic, between sexual attraction and lasting love. Happily married couples often say that they were made for each other, but they were not. They did *find* each other, and discerned a good fit—but so did other couples, who ended up divorcing. God does not manipulate us like puppets, nor does the universe focus its energies on every decision we make. We can blame neither

God nor the stars for our decisions. The most we can say in advance of such a journey is that we are as ready for it as we can be, and that the winds seem favorable.

So then, where is God in this? If God doesn't plan out our every move in advance, or send us clues by means of which we can ascertain the divine will, is there even such a *thing* as being called? If God is not orchestrating our lives, how *is* God present in the choices we make?

We can begin to sense a path through these questions when we remember that God is not imprisoned in the linear time we experience. If God experienced time the way we do, the notion of God's plan would make sense: there would be the divine equivalent of clocks and calendars in heaven. God would chart things, and then they would happen. God would experience the absence of things in the before-and-after, one-thing-after-another way we do.

But there can be no absence of being in the One who is the ground of all existence. There can only be *now*. So the planning part of God's presence in the world isn't necessary. It's not necessary that God *cause* things in order to be present in them. Our puzzling and daydreaming, then jerking ourselves awake and finally deciding—that *is* the plan. It is not foreknown. It is simultaneously known.

Our process itself *is* the call.

The call about which I am best informed is my own, which is the call to priesthood. But then again, I am also a writer. I have always viewed my writing as a call within a call, one way among the many ways of my being a priest. That is one of the nice things about the priesthood: it is general. Priests don't do just one thing. You accompany people through life, in all its stages and all its locations. There is no place in which there can be no opportunity to bless, no situation in which it is impossible to be a blessing, no person in whom the image of God is absent—though it can be hard to see in some of us.

Would I have had the opportunity to do and be these things if I were not a priest? Well, of course—the chance to be a blessing belongs to all of us. Could I have done something else? Sure. But after all these years, I can't imagine what.

The first section of this book is about my calling, the priesthood. It isn't about me specifically, though I appear in it from time to time—it's about the calling itself. For a number of years, I have led retreats for people about to be ordained in the Episcopal Diocese of New York. We go to a convent or a monastery just a few days before their ordination and spend twenty-four hours together. I've always told them I was going to put these talks together in a book, and now I have.

The second section attempts, in a very small way, to do justice to just a handful of other human callings. There are so many callings, and most of them are lay callings, while fewer than 1 percent of people of faith are ordained. The life of faith isn't just about the clergy. It's about everybody. We're all called to something.

**PART ONE**

# THE DREAM
# OF THE PRIEST

# 1
# THE DREAM OF THE PRIEST

**I STILL DREAM SOMETIMES THAT I** can fly. Flying is really easy—you surmount the tops of houses and sail over them, looking down at the roof tiles and chimneys as they pass beneath you. Maybe you approach a grove of trees, a bit cowed by their great height. Then you remember that you can fly, and your troubles are over: you float above them all. Funny, I never dream of landing—only of the ascent. I always awaken from these dreams a little surprised to be earthbound.

Let's see: a ballerina. An archeologist. A lawyer. A college professor. A singer. An actor. I thought I might be a lot of things. Priest was not on the radar screen for girls when I was young, so when I raised it as a possibility I was told that girls couldn't be priests, and I accepted that as the fact it was. I know many women priests who yearned to be ordained long before it was possible, but I was not one of them. There were plenty of other things to be.

I crowded some of these ambitions together at the same time—a career combining ballet and archeology made perfect sense to me for at least a year. I remember a friend in my dance class who wanted to be both a dancer and a nun. Why not, we told each other? The world was so full of interesting things to be, and our energy was boundless—we could not recall ever having been tired. Time seemed endless to us. In short, nothing stood in the way of our doing anything we wanted to do. This we knew. We were eleven or twelve, I think. Not enough of our lives had passed yet to sober us. Young girls think they can do anything.

Even after that golden I'll-have-one-of-everything phase is over, another invincible season follows, one in which it seems that a person can do anything she sets her mind to. That limits aren't real; they are merely a failure of nerve. I wish everybody could feel that way forever, but nobody does. Life is just not like that.

Eventually, you settle on something, in a more informed choice. Maybe you meet someone who already does that to which you aspire. Probably you seek out such people, make it your business to meet as many of them as you can, gravitating toward everything about this profession on which you are in the process of setting your heart.

Perhaps there are special clothes and equipment—a uniform, a lab coat. A stethoscope, perhaps. For us, a clerical collar and liturgical vestments. There are special stores that sell only clerical furnishings, and a quiet but rather intense rivalry exists among these establishments in their competition for the largest share of what has always been a very small market.

A flat package arrives at the door. You know what it

is—you've been expecting it, with an eagerness that would embarrass you if you thought anybody else knew about it. It is your new black clerical shirt, your first. With it, three round white collars and a set of collar studs—soon, you will have to order more studs, but you don't know that yet. You don't know how easy they are to lose.

You wait until you are alone to try it on—you don't really want anyone else to know that your appearance matters to you. You are a bit surprised yourself, actually; surely it was the work itself to which you were called, not the clothes. Occasionally, you have heaped inner scorn upon people you thought were too attracted to the haberdashery of your calling; now you appear to be one of them. And yet you study yourself in the mirror, once you've plumbed the intricacies of fastening the collar onto the shirt, an operation that was second nature to gentlemen of the Victorian era and will very soon be second nature to you. Something like a cleric looks back at you, somebody dressed in a way people don't dress any more, and never did, really: although well-dressed men of the nineteenth century did wear detachable collars, the round "dog collar" is not ancient, nor is it a survival of street wear from an earlier age, as so many liturgical vestments are. It dates only from the 1840s, and only clerics have ever worn it. Before 1840, the clergy dressed like everyone else. So did doctors, until even later, and nurses as well.

You don't know yet how often you will wear yours. You haven't learned yet that if you forget to pack your collar on a trip, you can make one out of stiff paper folded lengthwise, or from plastic you have cut in a strip from a white jug of laundry detergent. You don't know yet that you can fabricate a collar stud from a paper clip, if one of yours drops irretrievably down a grate, or that you can use a cufflink.

There is some other stuff you don't know yet.

My friend Kevin grew up Irish Catholic. He loved everything about church—the Latin, the incense, the music, the statues, the bread and the wine. Of course he was an altar boy. He was scrupulous in all his observances—a daily Mass and the daily confession that went with it, the keeping of every fast day. He loved all the priests in his parish, and was always available to serve them at the altar. It was apparent to him from before he made his First Holy Communion that he was born to be a priest, too, and everything in his life for as long as he could remember had been in preparation for that. His mother was proud—her son, a priest!

At seventeen, he was sent to minor seminary with the blessing of his entire Brooklyn neighborhood. Of course he loved it. He strove to excel in holiness, really to be the devout Catholic he knew God wanted him to be. He fasted more than other students, stayed in chapel longer after the liturgies had ended. Every day was a test, a chance to be better than he had been the day before.

Such devotion. I am guessing that he might have been a bit holier-than-thou with the other seminarians. Kevin was very young then, and young people aren't always as sensitive to the feelings of others as they might be.

The seminary years continued, and his devotion only increased, if that were possible. Certainly his professors' job was to encourage their students' piety, but even they grew concerned about Kevin's extreme version of it. It was too much! They forbade his extra fasts, his long chapel vigils. He needed to eat and sleep. The tussle between their concern and his devotion was an ongoing war. In time, Kevin lost. He was asked not to return.

He would never be a priest.

Kevin's dream was destroyed. The church to which he had dedicated his life had rejected his offering of himself. To say that he was devastated would be like saying that the Grand Canyon is big.

A long period of desolation followed. He found a secular career. He turned away from the church—it didn't help that these were the years in which the innovations of Vatican II were implemented, and Kevin couldn't stand any of them. The dignity and beauty he had loved all his life was swept away in a vernacular swirl of guitar music. It was clear that there was no church for him anymore.

Cutting this cord did open him to some things he had never considered. Love was one—he met the man who would become his life partner, and they began a relationship that would last more than fifty years. He lived a New York life, like millions of his fellow citizens—Sunday morning brunch with the *New York Times*. Years passed.

One day, Kevin was walking along West 46th Street on his way back to his office from lunch. He heard the music of an organ and looked in the direction from which it came, the open door of a church. He had passed that church a thousand times, but today the door was open. He climbed the steps and peered in: the priest was censing the altar, flanked by the deacon and subdeacon, who each lifted the hem of his beautiful brocade cope out of his way as he moved from one end of the altar to the other. Kevin could smell the incense from the door. He turned aside from his journey and walked in. The holy water stoup beside the entrance was full— he wet his fingers and crossed himself, for the first time in years. A statue of the Blessed Mother greeted him from behind her bank of votive candles in a station halfway down the nave.

The Mass was in English, yes, but it was Elizabethan English. It was not precisely the church of his childhood, but it was close enough. There was not a guitar in sight. Kevin was home.

The priest caught sight of him after the Mass and greeted him kindly. They talked for a few minutes that day, and Kevin hurried back to his office. But he began to attend Mass daily. He joined the parish. He did whatever he could to help out. No task was too big or too small. His partner was welcomed by the priest and everyone else when he visited. Kevin's Irish Catholic mother was dead by now, so she was spared the knowledge that her son was becoming an Episcopalian. This was a good thing, for it probably would have killed her.

The priest suggested that Kevin attend a Cursillo

retreat—the first one ever in Episcopal New York. He became a leader in that worldwide spiritual renewal community, founded and led by laypeople. This involved leadership at retreat weekends, where Kevin frequently was called upon to tell his story.

We heard this story often, over the years. Fifteen talks are given on a Cursillo weekend, and over the dozens of retreats in which he assisted, Kevin gave most of them, some more than once. This story of his vocation almost always made an appearance. Kevin revived his habit from seminary of staying in chapel (sometimes all night) to pray for people on the weekends, now an offering instead of scrupulosity. He was a mentor to many in the Cursillo movement in New York, as well as in his parish. From waiting on tables to presiding, he did it all gladly. He was a devoted and supportive friend to many priests and many laypeople, Episcopal and Roman Catholic alike. To tell this story, I reached out to friends from those days. We shared memories of Kevin, who has been dead for some time now. Writing about him here has made me miss him, and has filled me with gratitude for having known him.

Though they broke his heart, the faculty at the seminary were right about Kevin's vocation: he would have been the wrong kind of priest, he used to say, if he had realized his dream early in life as he and everyone else had expected he would. He would have regarded ordination as the reward for his rigid adherence to doing things the one and only right way. It would have confirmed him in the belief that perfection was not only possible, it was obligatory. Imposing it upon himself, he would have imposed it on others. He would have become harsh and judgmental. He would have been too dutiful to explore his own sexuality because of his vow of celibacy, and it would have ridden him painfully throughout his ministry.

But, you know—that's not the only alternative scenario to what happened in real life. Kevin and I both could have been wrong about the kind of priest he would have been. Yes, he would have started out demanding perfection from himself and everyone else. But he wouldn't have gotten it— and maybe he would have changed his approach. He wouldn't have been the first young priest who needed to calm down a little. I look back on my own early years now, and see an arrogance that embarrasses me just thinking about it. Because I was academically strong, I was overconfident, certain that I knew what was right. I didn't fully appreciate the fact that there are *fashions* in ministry, that practices and approaches come in and out of vogue, so I accepted the truisms of the time as both universal and eternal truths, when none of them were either of those.

So Kevin never did become a priest. But he showed us all what a lay leader could be. Could we say, then, that this outcome was "meant to be"? That it was part of God's plan for Kevin? The older I get, the less confident I am in my ability to identify God's plan, and the less attracted I am to the idea that God maps out plans for us, the way a general draws up a battle plan. Rather, it seems to me that God offers possibilities at every turn, opportunities to help a new thing happen in the world. A cherished goal becomes suddenly and permanently out of reach—and life doesn't end. Now something else can happen. Maybe Kevin would have been a good priest. Maybe he wouldn't have. But neither of those possibilities were inevitable: they were *possible*. Lately I've been thinking that *possible* is one of my favorite words.

Whom did you tell first, when the possibility of your vocation first became clear to you? Do you remember when it was? For some people, it is a stunning moment of call they remember for the rest of their lives: the moment, the day, where they were, what they were doing. For most, though, it is a process. We come to it inch by inch, not all at once. It becomes possible, not certain. Whom did you tell? Someone who loved you? Maybe. But maybe not. Sometimes we don't go to family first with something that's going to change our lives—they want our lives to stay the same. Family often can't see us as something other than what we already are. Sometimes family is the last to know.

More often than not, the one to whom you entrust the news of your vocation is the one who inspired you to it in the first place, if that person is still around. Or someone else who now does that work. I think most of us have a string of such people, not just one; we gravitate toward those who inhabit already the fellowship we long to join. We meet as many of them as we can.

The people you admire weren't always the experienced elders they are now. They all were once as you are now—they were new. They didn't always know all they know now—they had to learn it, as everyone must. They remember what it was like not to know. Perhaps one of them sees something familiar in you. *I was like that*, he or she may remember, and there is a growing warmth to your interactions. When the time does come for you to tell someone what has been growing in your heart, this is the person you seek out. *Do I have what it takes? Can you imagine me in this role? What should I do first?*

Notice that I didn't say anything about *Is God calling me to do this?*

I cannot know what God is or is not doing. None of us can. I especially can't know this when what I am discerning involves my own passionate desire—human beings easily confuse our own desires with God's will. We also anthropomorphize God scandalously; we think God is just like us, only omnipotent—sort of like Superman. That God likes and desires things in the same way we do. We use language about God like the people in the Bible used, thinking that in doing so we are being faithful to the Scriptures, when what we are really doing is confining God to the thought processes of a particular time and place. We do not allow God to do new things, when the very essence of God is *to create*. God is the creator, not the replicator.

So I can't know if God is calling you to be a priest. Or to be a teacher or a waiter or a nurse or an engineer. All I can judge is whether or not you have the qualities I know to be useful in a calling, if it's one about which I am well-informed. Scornful of those less knowledgeable than you are? Probably not a teacher. Faint at the sight of blood? Something other than nursing, maybe. We can expect God to use what is already present to form us, and we can expect that God's call will probably not be a violation of who we are. It will be *in line* with who we are. The best indicator of a vocation may be that the people who know you aren't surprised when you tell them about it—they've already seen it in you.

And what they have seen is not just aptitude. Vocation is never only potential—it is actual. It is recognizable before it appears in full. Insofar as has been possible, you've already been exercising your vocation, even before you begin your formal training for it.

But, although your vocation won't be in violation of who you are, it could be in violation of who you *think* you are. We don't see ourselves as clearly as we imagine we do. I remember a young man who swore he would never become a priest. Anything but that. His father was one, and worked at night a lot. He would never do that to *his* family. Naturally, he went on to become a priest, and naturally, he found ways to be the father he wanted to be.

Sometimes the world sees the initial outline of your vocation before you do. Other times the part of the world you need to see it fails to do so. Sometimes this doesn't matter—you can just go forward anyway, on your own. But usually, it matters a great deal. In the church, for instance, there are gatekeepers, and they must agree with you that a vocation exists. In the church as Episcopalians have inherited it, discernment is a threefold action of the Holy Spirit: upon me, upon my community, and upon my bishop. It is not something we do as individuals—we do it together. Somehow, we must all agree that we are seeing the same thing in me, or we do not proceed.

And there are *trends* in the church's attitude toward vocation, trends that come and go. When I was studying, most of my classmates were young, as I was. Early in my priesthood, though, it began to seem to many in authority that younger aspirants needed to get some real world experience before beginning, and more than a few excellent ones were turned down solely on the basis of not being old enough, never to return to the process. I have lived to see this come full circle—right now, very young people are the prize in diocesan discernment processes, and it is the middle-aged who must explain themselves. When I was beginning, parish ministry was the gold standard, and anyone who aspired to anything else, such as chaplaincy in a hospital or a school—and made the mistake of saying so—could live to regret it. At the moment, there is somewhat more flexibility in this regard. Tomorrow, who knows? Although one might consider it crass to say so, the inexorable law of supply and demand is as active in the ordination process as it is elsewhere, necessitating flexibility at the front end when priests are in short supply. When there are too many for the positions available, the church is choosier. It can fail to see some gems because they don't fit the mold.

Though this looks to people involved in the discernment process like a thoroughly regrettable contraction in possibilities, it is important to remember that there is no such thing as contraction of possibility in the reality of God. God doesn't contract; God expands. The creation is ongoing and the universe is getting bigger; the individual deaths we mourn—the deaths of stars, of galaxies, to say nothing of our own little deaths—are compost for a larger growth. As in the universe, so in the church: that there aren't as many positions now like the one I had after seminary—as curate under the supervision of an experienced rector—does not mean there is no need for priests to gather the people of God, only that we will do it in a different way. It is at just such times that the imagination of God makes something new.

Back when the ordination of women was news, not many parishes were willing to take a chance on hiring one. All of us remember hearing a regretful "My people aren't ready for a woman" and wondering silently just what the sign of the people's readiness would be. We were suspicious of the expressed regret; we heard it as "I am not ready, but am not willing to admit it—so I will blame it on my congregation." Looking back now, from the perspective of someone who has had to balance conflicting viewpoints on controversial issues in a parish many times, this was a bit harsh—there was more truth in what they said than I was prepared to admit. Almost any rector who hired a woman was certain to face opposition from some of his parishioners, and would have to navigate his way through it. *Parish ministry is hard enough; do I really want to invite a conflict that might destroy the fragile balance I've worked so hard to maintain?* The parish rebellions they imagined before the fact were more severe in the imagining than they turned out to be in real life, but then we never do know what something is going to be like until we try it. Trying it took guts. Still, it was hard on us to watch our male classmates find full-time positions in prosperous churches with relative ease, while we struggled to locate places that might let us work for free.

What this meant was that women were in a position to understand from personal experience something of what it had been like for African American and other minority clergy for two centuries. The same went for openly gay clergy, who were just beginning to claim their truth out loud in those days. There were just places none of us could go, for reasons that had nothing to do with our fitness to serve.

After an appropriate moment or two of outrage and hurt, though, a person in that position still must find a place in which to exercise the vocation to which we are called. *Okay,* you must find a way to say to yourself, *so we know what I can't do right now. Let's see what I* can *do.* Some women strung together two or three part-time positions. Some worked at secular jobs and served parishes as non-stipendiary clergy on the weekends. Some created parish positions that had not existed before, and the men in charge of those parishes helped them do it. Most of these men were very aware of the economic injustice of all this, and troubled by the ethical dilemma confronting them: which is worse, allowing a woman to work here for little or no money, or not allowing her to work at all? But most of us wanted to work, no matter what we were paid. We hoped and trusted that the scales would balance better in the future. And balance they did, after a fashion, with about the same tilt the general culture displays: more and more women found full-time positions in parishes as time went by, but once they passed the moment when diocesan minimum salaries apply, women enjoyed roughly the same seventy cents on the dollar ratio to men's salaries prevalent in the secular world. It may be a little better now, but not much.

Nope, it isn't fair. Still, the result has been that some very gifted women serve in places that wouldn't have been able to afford them if they had been men. Seeing all this has led me unwillingly to an observation I still believe: there are some positive benefits to limited opportunity. It forces us into places we would not have chosen on our own. Once there, we discover gifts in parishes in which we never would have imagined ourselves. This doesn't mean that we shouldn't keep trying to even the playing field. It only means that NO is never the last word in ministry. There will always be a dependable supply of clergy wanting to serve rich parishes. Not everyone can serve in a poor one—it is hard work, and your resources are few. Those of us who can, probably should.

Not getting what we want isn't the worst thing that can

happen to us. No. The worst thing would be to let it keep us from using what we have.

Sally had loved theology since before she was old enough to know what it was. Puzzling about where things came from, about both the immensity and the tiny-ness of the natural world, sitting on the rock she has thought of as hers since her childhood on the coast of Maine and watching the sea change with the tides—these were both deep delights and spiritual quests for a curious little girl. She was also rather more abundantly churched than many people, dutifully attending the Congregational church of her parents early on Sunday mornings and then going with her grandfather to the Episcopal church after that. The more sensual beauty of the liturgy there—even in that plainer liturgical era—struck a chord in her, and its effect on her grandfather intrigued and attracted her. The way his face changed as the service unfolded, she said—he became so full of peace.

Fast forward: a life in the arts, a family, busy decades as an active Episcopalian—then the breast cancer nobody ever expects visited her. A chaplain's ministry to her in the hospital saved her spiritual life and maybe her sanity, she thought, and she realized that she wanted to be able to bring that to other people. It seemed of one fabric with everything else she had known of God throughout her life—the wonder of nature, the deep peace of prayer, the beauty of liturgy.

Maybe it was her age—Sally was not a twenty-something. Probably her clarity about a vocation to hospital chaplaincy worked against her. "Maybe I'm just not good at communicating who I am to people," she says now. I wasn't there, so I don't know. However it was, she was not invited to continue exploring an ordained vocation.

She completed a seminary degree anyway—nobody could stop her from learning. She completed several units of clinical pastoral education, the training required of hospital chaplains. She accepted a position as pastoral care assistant to the rector in her parish, one she held for seven years. Then she became a hospice chaplain at a residential facility for older adults. She taught seminars in end-of-life issues to medical students at Yale. She became a spiritual director to seminary students, both at Princeton and at Yale.

"So then, you got to do all the things you wanted to do," I said, "even though you never were ordained?"

Sally paused. "I did. But it was harder. You see, when you have the recognition ordination confers, people *assume* you're a good pastor."

"Even if you're really *not* very good at it."

"Exactly. But if you're not ordained, you have to prove it up front, every time."

"Yeah. We assume that ordained people are pastors, and that laypeople *aren't*."

"Exactly."

That's the truth. All credentials are shorthand. Each certifies a certain level of mastery—there are things every lawyer must know, things every accountant must be able to do, and the initials "JD" or "CPA" after one's name signal to the world that such mastery is present.

Credentials signify professional consensus: *Not only do I think I'm qualified, the people already recognized in my chosen profession do, too. I undertook a course of study and completed it. I sat for an examination and passed it.*

There is nothing wrong with requiring credentials. Any profession has every reason to maintain rigorous standards for its members; its failure to do so would injure everybody in it and cast rightful aspersions on the profession itself. To the extent that the care of souls is a profession, it is right that we cannot simply appoint ourselves to it.

But there is an inevitable lack of precision to the credentialing process in many professions. Maybe in most of them. Strive though we may to be "objective," many factors combine to inform our judgments of one another. A candidate looks or sounds like your mother, went to a school that was your school's rival, believes something other than you believe about something that matters greatly to you. You yourself are not feeling well today, or you are deeply worried about something completely unrelated to the candidate before you. I will set these things aside, you say, and you think you have. But the heart has many layers, and not all of them are known to us.

Also, judgments are local. Attitudes toward controversial topics vary from place to place. A lesbian candidate in the Episcopal Diocese of New York need not conceal that important fact about herself from the committee that examines her. There are still many dioceses in which that is far from being the case. When I was taking the General

Ordination exam, which is required of all candidates for the priesthood and is administered anonymously, women students were advised to write in such a way that our gender was not apparent—our readers would come from all over the country, and the ordination of women was unwelcome news in many places. Gay men from that era recall being advised to refer to their same-sex partners by the opposite gender's pronoun. It seemed an odd way to begin a life in which they would vow to follow Someone who was "the way, the truth, and the life." But I knew more than one person whose ordination didn't happen because they couldn't bring themselves to lie.

So there is nothing inevitable about being called, to ordained ministry or to anything else. Imagining that being called to ministry means you're certain to be ordained is like imagining that being a good Christian means you'll never get cancer. Many factors can contradict your sense of call, however certain it may seem to you. The thread of Providence is not discernible from the beginning, only from the end. All we are equipped to see are gifts, talents, and a natural tilt toward exercising them.

Your life's calling does not need to be ordained beforehand in order to be your life's calling. Indeed, in the reality of God, there can *be* no "beforehand" or "afterward." Everything is "now" in the reality of God. The linearity of the human experience of time is ours alone—if God is the ground of all existence, then God has the capacity to hold all things at once, rather than stringing them out along a line, as we must do in order to experience them. I have written rather extensively elsewhere about time and history as God sees it, and so have many others. When we separate God from our experience of God, we actually reduce the divine nature: God becomes simply a better player on the same field in which we play, the captain of our team, larger and stronger than we are, but a player, as we are players. It is when we understand ourselves to be part of God's incarnation—to be what Paul calls "in Christ"—that the trajectory of our own intention and that of the universe click into alignment. In that alignment is the energy that can birth new things.

We think God makes choices the way we make choices—*I will do this, so I will not do that*. God seems either/or to us because we experience ourselves as either/or. But even we are more complex than that, in every avenue of our lives. The love of your life isn't the only person you could possibly have married—he is just the one you *did* marry. The building of your life together continued to marry the two of you, day by day. Likewise, the children you bore or fathered were not fulfilled in purpose simply by being born to you: a decision to father or mother them you made daily for years created your parenthood as you went along. Adoptive families demonstrate this: adoptive parents are certainly parents, and birth parents may elect not to be. A family can be created without the usual beginning—the conception of a child together. The reverse is also true—the usual beginning does not always produce a family.

Sally's vocation as a chaplain was like this. Denied the usual beginning to a ministry of chaplaincy, she reached it by an alternate route. If credentials like ordination are shorthand, Sally's vocation was written longhand. Doing it that way was harder, but since it was the only one available to her, she accepted it. In almost every way, she lived her calling. *Almost* every way: what was missing was the ease of entry into it, based on evidence that a community supported her. Ordination gives us that, but Sally had to secure it afresh each time, with the only evidence of a good job well done provided in the facilities' performance evaluations, which were internal documents. The other evidence, provided by the patients and families and staff with whom she worked in one setting, was also not readily available to any new one. This is true, later on, for the ordained as well, of course—your collar may get you in the door, but it won't keep you there if the competence and faithfulness it promises are nowhere to be found. The beginning is not the end. There are people for whom the day of their ordination represents the high point of their ministry. Certainly, that was a memorable day—let's hope, though, that it was not your high point. If I were to ask someone to tell me about his priesthood after he'd served for forty years and what he told me about was the first day of it, I would try my best to hide my horror. But I would probably fail.

Naïve though it may be, the ideal which attracts us to priesthood is a powerful lure, potent enough to keep us on the long road toward it, in spite of the obstacles we encounter. Paradoxically, we must be prepared to begin surrendering the ideal as soon as we are ordained. The ideal of your vocation was formed primarily through observation, but your actual vocation is created through experience. We make it by living it. There is no way to know in advance just what it will be like, and there is only one way to find out.

Finding out will be disruptive. Not everyone fights it as hard as my friend Vicki did. Her understanding of her call is different from mine—it comes from a God unmistakably outside herself:

> I was already a concert organist, teaching associate in organ and music theory, and organist and choir director. My goal was a tenure track position, as well as concertizing and encouraging composers to write new compositions for the organ.
>
> Call for me meant a total change of profession, going back to school and starting all over. I fought it as hard as I could. My father, uncles, grandfathers, and great-grandfather were all pastors in the Missouri Synod Lutheran Church, a denomination that still does not accept the ordination of women, so this was not something I considered as a young girl.
>
> I began working at an Episcopal Church as their organist and choir director when my Jewish husband's father was diagnosed with a

brain tumor. That year of struggling with life and death issues in a vibrant community of faith was transformative, and the "coincidences" that kept happening provided solace and love in such a deep way that they could not be easily discarded as "chance." A very specific mystical experience had me wondering if God was calling me to ordained ministry. I began sessions with a spiritual director, but was able to rationalize that I already had a doctorate in music and that my music career used all of my gifts and talents. The first anniversary of that experience, however, was a terrible day because I knew that I was supposed to change my life and I hadn't.

I was angry with God for changing the rules, for the sexism and sexual harassment I had endured in academia, and for my own deep-seated fear of stepping into a brand new patriarchal system about which I knew nothing. The answer I heard from God was that it wouldn't be easy but that Christ would always be with me. I went through a few more months of crying and agony until I finally gave in.

The experience of fighting a call is not an experience I know; mine was gentler than Victoria's, and it did not involve as much disruption. But many prophets of ancient

Israel knew it well; the most famous among them argued strenuously with God at the moment of their calling. Here is Moses:

> But Moses said to the LORD, "O my Lord, I have never been eloquent, neither in the past nor even now that you have spoken to your servant; but I am slow of tongue." Then the LORD said to him, "Who gives speech to mortals? Who makes them mute or deaf, seeing or blind? Is it not I, the LORD? Now go, and I will be with your mouth and teach you what you are to speak." But he said, "O my Lord, please send someone else."
>
> Exodus 4:10–13

And here is Isaiah:

> And I said: "Woe is me! I am lost, for I am a man of unclean lips, and I live among a people of unclean lips; yet my eyes have seen the king, the LORD of hosts!" Then one of the seraphs flew to me, holding a live coal that had been taken from the altar with a pair of tongs. The seraph touched my mouth with it and said: "Now that this has touched your lips, your guilt has departed and your sin is blotted out." Then I heard the voice of the LORD saying, "Whom shall I send, and who will go for us?" And I said, "Here am I; send me!"
>
> Isaiah 6:5–8

Jeremiah:

> Now the word of the LORD came to me saying,
> "Before I formed you in the womb I knew you,
> and before you were born I consecrated you; I
> appointed you a prophet to the nations." Then I
> said, "Ah, Lord GOD! Truly, I do not know how
> to speak, for I am only a boy." But the LORD said
> to me, "Do not say, 'I am only a boy'; for you shall
> go to all to whom I send you, and you shall speak
> whatever I command you.
>
> Jeremiah 1:4–7

Jonah:

> Now the word of the LORD came to Jonah son
> of Amittai, saying, "Go at once to Nineveh,
> that great city, and cry out against it; for their
> wickedness has come up before me." But Jonah
> set out to flee to Tarshish from the presence of
> the LORD. He went down to Joppa and found a
> ship going to Tarshish, away from the presence
> of the LORD.
>
> Jonah 1:1–3

As painful as coming to terms with the beginning of
Victoria's call to priesthood was, it was not her last uncomfortable era. The rigor of the work itself has remained
a challenge. "It has been the hardest journey I could ever

even imagine. It has involved working on my own spiritual discernment and struggling with the voices within me that would run away from God. I have had to find a more authentic and truthful humility, and deal with my fear of a living God. I have had to learn to pray for my enemies, and even to love them. I have had to put my ego aside again and again in order to hear that 'still small voice.' This has meant going places I didn't want to go, and doing things I don't necessarily want to do."

Here, precisely, is a sign of being called—the burden of ministry is hard to bear but, over and over, you are able to bear it. At the very moment when you realize that you have nothing to give, something within you is found. "But it is always in that most vulnerable and tender place," she says, "that I feel the presence and love of God most profoundly."

A sign of call like that cannot be found in the sunny meadows of easy success. Easy success only convinces us that we're great priests. A priceless sign such as this only surfaces when we come up empty.

Besides this unexpected strength in the hard times, more clear-cut rewards continue to hold Victoria.

There is nothing quite like knowing that you have just been used by God—that the words that came out of your mouth spoke to someone in such a deep way that they felt Christ's love for them and that that experience has changed their lives in some way. I have loved blessing and marrying couples, and am especially moved by working with same-sex couples and having the opportunity to apologize to them and their family and friends for the past sins of the church in shaming them and trying to take away from them their direct connection to God's love. I love baptizing babies, children and adults, preparing young people and adults for confirmation, reception, and reaffirmation. I love comforting people with prayer during times of trial. . . . And I love really knowing, despite all of the horrific things that happen in the world, God's "got the whole world in his hands."

When the biblical writers write of reluctant prophets, they show us impressive Cecil B. DeMille–style moments of triumph. They don't show us this part: the joy of knowing that you have answered the call and done your best, and that the energy of God's love has flowed quietly but unmistakably through you to touch those you serve. I am in exactly the right place and doing exactly what I was created to do, you say wonderingly to yourself.

Forty years later, you're still saying the same thing.

## AARON

Holiness on the head,
  Light and perfections on the breast,
Harmonious bells below, raising the dead
  To lead them unto life and rest:
    Thus are true Aarons drest.

Profaneness in my head,
  Defects and darkness in my breast,
A noise of passions ringing me for dead
  Unto a place where is no rest:
    Poor priest thus am I drest,

Only another head
  I have, another heart and breast,
another music, making live, not dead,
  without whom I could have no rest:
    In him I am well drest.

Christ is my only head,
  My alone-only heart and breast,
My only music, striking me ev'n dead;
  That to the old man I may rest,
    And be in him new-drest.

So, holy in my head,
  Perfect and light in my dear breast,
My doctrine tun'd by Christ, (who is not dead,
  But lives in me while I do rest),
    Come people; Aaron's drest.

George Herbert, 1633

George Herbert was an English priest. In this poem, he contrasts his own unworthiness with the high calling of his ministry, represented through references to the vestments Aaron wore, which are described in great detail in scripture—you can read about his splendid apparel in the twenty-eighth chapter of Exodus. Aaron is a type of priesthood in both Judaism and Christianity; a fact most modern people don't know but which would not have been lost on anyone in Herbert's day. Herbert served the tiny church of St. Andrew in Bemerton. As modest as it was, his sense of his own unworthiness to serve it save by the power of God's presence was potent. He spent the night before he was to take it up stretched out on its stone floor in prayer over his unworthiness.

## 2
# THE PRIEST IN THE DESERT

**I LOOK BACK AT MY EARLY** years and see mostly my mistakes. As a matter of fact, I look back on my entire ministry and see mostly my mistakes. The reason for that is partly a morose temperament, but mostly it is because those lessons were indelible—we have no better teacher than our own failures. Even when the sting is gone, we don't forget how it felt.

So we should treasure the times we fell on our faces. Every one of them carried a lesson for us—mostly, how not to do things. Things you should never do. Things you should never fail to do. Things you should never assume, which is pretty much everything. Some of these lessons are so obvious they would not have escaped my three-year-old granddaughter—I once took a youth group roller-skating and left one of them behind there when we left. His parents were pretty peeved. I told a friend who was a schoolteacher, hoping for some sympathy. "Count heads," was all she said. I've been counting heads ever since.

Other things we learn from failure are less clear. I had a friend at the gas station—he was always jovial when I pulled in for a tank of gas, always asked after my colleague. If I left the car for an oil change, he'd give me a lift back to the church. He was not a member of the church, but I liked it that we were friends—I could see that he respected my orders, and our easy, bantering relationship somehow made me feel like I must be a good priest.

Of course, I was very new in the business.

I pulled in for some gas one day on my way to a meeting in Newark. We passed the time of day as he filled the tank. Where was I going?

"Up to Newark. Got a meeting up there."

"I don't never go up there. There's too many niggers up there."

He said it easily, the way we always spoke to each other. Said it just as if he'd said something about the weather, or about baseball. We were friends. I liked him and he liked me. Probably I'd agree with him about there being too many niggers in Newark. I felt the blood drain from my face. I gathered myself and said something silly, something like "Now, now!" or "Oh, come on!" in a mock scolding way. As if I thought he'd been joking. As if *I* were joking. I paid for the gas and drove away.

I never went back to his gas station again. I would see him at the pumps sometimes as I passed by—I wondered if he saw me, and if he ever wondered why I never stopped in anymore. If he did, I know he didn't connect my absence with our last conversation. Why would he? Nothing in my behavior would have caused him to do so.

I didn't call him on it. I didn't ask him to tell me why he felt that way. Didn't tell him that language like that was degrading to use and degrading to hear. I had a chance to use that moment as a way to help my friend grow, and I didn't seize it. I had a chance to stand up for what is right, and I didn't do it. I didn't do any of those things. I just said something glib and then I ran away. I wasn't his friend, not really—that had been nothing more than a pretty little self-portrait I painted, a self-congratulatory fable about my own magnanimous reach across class differences. No. I was no friend to that man. I was too much of a coward to call myself his friend.

But I did learn from that failure. I learned that prophecy is easy in front of a crowd and hard in a one-to-one encounter. I learned that not to sidle away from a chance to stand for what is right takes guts, and a tougher kind of love than I knew about in those days.

I failed to live up to my ideal. You will fail to live up to your ideal, too, and you will fail many times. Many times, you will not be the priest you know you could be, should be—the priest you want to be. You will be weary, or angry, or in the grip of something you do not understand. Nothing is more important than that you be corrected, no matter how painful the correction. Getting away with it could kill you.

Somebody you know and like will crash and burn. Somebody will do something outside the pale, something that cannot be written off or explained away. Something against the law, perhaps. Something so utterly unlike the person you thought you knew that at first you don't believe it's true. It may be somebody to whom you are very close. It may be more than one person, throughout the long years of your career—odds are, there will be more than one. It may even be you.

D was my best friend in seminary. Actually, I think he was a lot of people's best friend—D had that effect on everyone. But we did spend a lot of time together: breakfast, lunch, and supper in the refectory, under the watchful eyes of the deceased faculty members whose darkened portraits lined the walls. Dinner out, sometimes, as our wallets allowed. Chelsea in the 1970s was not the boutiquey New York neighborhood it is today, and good restaurants there were few and far between. But there were always the Empire Diner and Moran's, and they were beginning to convert some of the old warehouses on 11th Avenue into loft apartments and restaurants. Or just coffee in D's room after class. *Come on up for a cup of sludge*, he would say most midmornings, and he would brew us cups of coffee so strong a spoon could have stood upright in them. We would sit and talk for about an hour, and then get back to work.

D wasn't the best student in our class, though he certainly wasn't the worst—D was in the middle. He was clear about his goals in this regard: *I do as well as I need to do,* he told me once, and I admired his realism. It contrasted markedly with my own competitiveness about school, a competitiveness I did my best to hide, thinking it unbecoming in a theology student to be so concerned with my scores. He was right, of course—seminary is the only place where anybody is going to care about your grades. Your bishop won't care, as long as you do well enough to graduate and pass your exams. The people in your parish won't care—they have more reliable ways of discerning your fitness. If you're going to do all the hard work necessary to have *cum laude* inscribed on your diploma, it had better be for your own satisfaction, because nobody else is going to pay it any mind.

D may not have been the academic star of our class, but I do think he was the most beloved. Or maybe I'm wrong about that—looking back now, I see many people who were beloved. We were, after all, a group of people whose calling in life would be to love. And D had that gift: he was easy to love. He was remarkably at ease with everyone he met. It was in the human interaction of ministry that he shone. He was a wonderful listener. His self-deprecating humor made you feel as if you could tell him anything, and people did.

We would miss each other when we graduated, we knew. We pledged to stay close, of course, and at first we did. We served as curates in parishes about half an hour apart on the train, he in a troubled city and I in a leafy suburban town. I visited his parish and he visited mine. We had lunch, talked on the phone. It was easy to stay in touch. But then he became rector of a church on the Main Line of Philadelphia, and I, against the advice of everyone who loved me except for D, became a chaplain to merchant seafarers on the New York waterfront.

Once in a while, a lunch. Once in a while, a phone call. But we were both so busy! Once, I remember, we did somehow find the time to schedule a dinner, and I was excited to be seeing him again. But when I arrived at the restaurant, he didn't show—his partner was there, along with some other friends, but no D. The explanation his partner gave for his absence escapes my memory now, but I do recall thinking that it didn't quite hang together. Oh well, I thought, why had I imagined that things would stay the same? Of course there would be new best friends, especially for someone like D. Our lives had moved on.

More time passed, and another pair of vocational changes for us: we each accepted calls to large parishes in New York City. This will be great, we told each other on the phone. New York! It will be just like the old days.

But it wasn't. The quick subway trips for lunch, that would have been so easy now, just didn't happen. Year gave way to year, with only the occasional D sighting, always accidental. I was always glad to see him, as he was always glad to see me. But of course, I told myself, things do change.

A clergy luncheon, one day, at my place. D never came to those, but a colleague of his was there. On that day, the colleague was bristling with indignation: one of their priests had embezzled money from a former parish, he had learned. And it was to support a cocaine habit, which was still active. "No wonder he never has any money," he growled. "Every time I have lunch with him I end up with the tab."

"Wait," I said. I had been talking to the person on my left. "Who did you say that was?"

"DH."

"DH?" I couldn't believe my ears. I strained to hear something other than what had been said. "DH, you say?"

"Yes, DH." He looked at me strangely. "Do you know him?"

"Well, yes. That is . . . do you mean the DH who went to General Seminary?" This was a dumb question: the Episcopal Church is a small town, and Episcopal New York is even smaller. There weren't two people named DH serving churches in Manhattan. I was still desperately casting around for an alternate narrative, but there were none to be had. We were talking about my D.

Some memories from our youth came back to me then. The missed dinner party. The time I suggested a cup of sludge in his room and he put me off, saying he had had a party the night before and the place was a mess. I told him I couldn't care less what his place looked like, and he came back at me, repeating his refusal with an edge of insistence in his voice—unlike him. I now think there must have been some paraphernalia there he didn't want me to see.

He had taken a lot of money from the church on the Main Line. He and his partner had to mortgage their house to repay what he had stolen. The church did not press charges. Thus, his reputation was intact, but so was his addiction. As soon as he could, D escaped to New York. He was still wonderful, still lovable; the cover-up skills that life as an addict had taught him served him every bit as well in the new place, and he was soon as indispensable and as beloved there as he had been everywhere else he had served.

In time, his successor at the old church found out about the whole thing and blew the whistle, insisting that the wardens notify the church where he was serving now. That was probably the best thing anybody ever did for D, although I doubt he thought so at the time.

I wrote to his rector. *I know this is terrible*, I wrote, *but please remember who he is. Remember all the things he has been, and can be still. Those things are all still true, even though we now know some other things to be true as well.*

What happened next would not have happened if all this had taken place in our own liability-conscious era, when our every decision is haunted by the possibility of being sued for whatever it is we are contemplating. Today, D would be fired immediately, walked to the door by security, and never again seen on the premises. But this was a long time ago. He wasn't fired. The rector insisted he go to a rehab, and decided to wait until he had done so before making a decision about whether to keep him on.

D hated the rehab, his discouraged partner told me on the phone. The people there were losers. He said the group meetings were a stupid waste of time. They were doing him no good at all. Time went by, though, and the wisdom of the rooms began to penetrate his defenses. He completed the course of treatment and began a new life in recovery. And his position at the church was waiting for him when he came out.

The church was full of successful people—a priest who was a drug addict and a thief wasn't what they had been raised to expect. Who knew what their reaction would be upon his return? For the most part, they surprised themselves—a few did leave in righteous indignation, muttering darkly about what the church was coming to these days. But most stayed. They still loved him. He was still funny, compassionate, open-hearted D, only now he was even more so—whatever parts of him his demon had stolen from the world were restored to it. When the rector retired, D spoke at the farewell dinner: "You saved my life," he said simply. And everyone there knew what he meant.

Though the deception was over, there was still more pain to come. Who can say what risky behavior D had gotten into over the years of his addiction? Over lunch, he told me the story of his first interview with the rector who followed the one who had saved his life.

"So the first time he learned that I was gay was also when I told him I had AIDS."

"Wow. How did it go?"

"I thought he took it well."

I guess he did. D became the new rector's right hand, as he had been for the previous one. He brought with him the same administrative skill, the same institutional memory, the same love of the congregation he had always brought. He stayed for years—he stayed for the rest of his life, in fact. As his illness worsened, he worked for as long as he could, and then he retired on disability. Even after that, he worked for a few hours a week as a volunteer. He preached on Sundays when he could. The people learned from him that it's never too late, no matter who you are and no matter what you've done. They learned that it is not only in our success that

God's grace is revealed. It can be revealed even more powerfully in our failure.

"Hey, know how to get a standing ovation?"

"How?"

"Just get up in the pulpit and tell them you're a thief and a crack addict and have AIDS."

"Yeah?"

"Well, it worked for me."

By this time, he had a port in his arm, so that the injections he needed so often would be easier to administer. His face and body were covered with skin tags. He had a necrotizing infection in one hip—"I know I'm supposed to be dying, but this is ridiculous. How can my hip die before the rest of me?"

I returned from a holiday in the British Virgin Islands to find a note on my computer keyboard. *Call Bill right away*, it read. I knew what had happened. The funeral would be in two days. I would assist. Bill sent out an e-mail asking everyone to give him D-isms we might remember, that he might be able to use in his sermon at the funeral. I e-mailed one back. *I remember that he always used to say, "Well, I must press on," whenever he had to leave a gathering.*

> But this one thing I do: forgetting what lies
> behind and straining forward to what lies ahead,
> I press on toward the goal for the prize of the
> heavenly call of God in Christ Jesus.
>
> Philippians 3:13–14

St. Paul, who wrote this, had spent the early part of his adult life persecuting the first Christians with great enthusiasm. He may even have collaborated in killing some of them. Not surprisingly, many people in the early church were indignant at Paul's presence in their midst later on, after he had been converted. They couldn't get beyond his past. But some could, and so Paul was enabled to become the apostle to the Gentiles, which is why Christianity spread throughout the Hellenized world instead of remaining a local sect of Judaism. If we can get beyond the worst thing a person has ever done, there is a whole person there to be discovered. *If you were his friend before, be his friend now*, a friend counseled a congregation about another leader who had fallen hard. Maybe that's hard to do. Maybe you're afraid that his public shame will be contagious: *What if people see us together and think that I was somehow in on what he did? Or at least, that I approve of it?* People stay away in droves when someone falls, heaping the pain of isolation atop the pain of the remorse already there. But if you can find it in your heart—and in your spine—not to disappear, you might be the means by which someone finds his way back home.

Sometimes, of course—well, *often*, come to think of it, maybe even *usually*—the one who falls *doesn't* feel remorse at all. He feels like a victim, not a perpetrator. He feels unfairly treated, misunderstood. He is apt to minimize or to justify his misdeed. Might not *this* be a good reason to stay away, then, until he's good and sorry?

I think not. He is still lost in the swamp of denial that

caused his fall in the first place. With no friend to confide in, he has no one with whom to begin the journey toward a more accurate understanding of himself. If all he hears from anyone is either condemnation or silence, where can he begin the pilgrimage away from the desperate tap dance of rationalization into which he now pours so much energy, energy that would be better spent coming to terms with reality? His resistance to the truth is a mechanism that shields him from the full weight of his own responsibility for the pain he is in, a desperate attempt to mold the truth into something less humiliating. It is easier to say that other people are narrow and judgmental than it is to admit that I have sinned greatly and am rightfully paying for it. Easier, but not truthful enough to trigger the healing that must take place if I am ever to be restored to the world. Am I likely to arrive at such truth on my own? I may not be. It is a fearsome task. The half-truth in which I have taken refuge is so much easier on me. But it may be that someone whose love I can depend on can help me get there, and that can only be a person who is willing to put up with my self-justification until it has run its sorry course.

J was the interim rector of St. C's before I went there as rector. He did a good job there, as he had done a good job in every interim situation he had taken on. Interim work is specialized—the congregation is sad at losing their beloved pastor, or else they were furious at him or her and are glad of the departure. Probably the congregation contains a mix of the two attitudes, as well as a few others. They may cherish dysfunctional behavior patterns that have held them back from growth and health for years. The interim pastor must help them get their bearings and prepare for a new life. J did this well. We had dinner together before I took up the leadership at St. C's so he could bring me up to date on things I needed to know, and he was helpful to me.

J was a star. He was brilliant, a fine scholar, a sought-after teacher and speaker. A wonderful preacher. He was the author of a number of books. But he was also kind to everyone, encouraging to a little church that had seen its share of reverses. His wife was a musician, and jumped right into the work of accompanying and encouraging the music. There were some difficult memories in the place, and J gently helped bring them to light, in a process that was necessary, though it was painful to some.

I received a phone call from the diocese one morning. They thought I ought to know something about J, as they knew many at St. C's had loved him. It seems that he had falsified portions of his vitae, and had done so in some odd ways—lied about when he had received his doctorate, about when and where he had been ordained, places in which he had served. Lied about some other things that I cannot now remember. He was being relieved of his current position and would be inhibited from serving elsewhere. Inhibition is what happens to a cleric when he or she is under ecclesiastical discipline for an offense—no leadership in a church, no sacramental acts, maybe other limitations. Often, it is an interim status while the bishop determines whether or not the cleric should be deposed from ordained ministry altogether.

This was hard to believe. Why? He was so gifted. J didn't need to manufacture qualifications. His work was so good, and he so widely and highly esteemed for it—why gild the lily? I thought of D right away. The two men were not at all alike. But I remembered the righteous indignation of his colleague that day, the steely curtain of silence that falls immediately upon the accused in a church setting. In any setting, for that matter. The one accused of wrongdoing is immediately radioactive. No one will go near him. I picked up the phone and called J.

I reminded him of all the good work he had done at St. C's, and that we would always be grateful. Could we have lunch? Yes, he said, that would be nice. So a date was made for the following week. But on the appointed day, a phone message—J couldn't make it, could we reschedule? I called back and got voice mail. But he didn't call back to make a new date. I made a couple of additional attempts, and then I let it go. I never heard from J again, and I don't know anybody else who has heard of him again. I heard he left the country.

J didn't want to have lunch with me. I'm guessing he didn't have lunch with anybody. I hope I'm wrong. We weren't close friends, after all—maybe there *was* somebody to whom he could turn with his truth, or even with his silence. But I suspect he just left the room. Just recently I searched for him on the Internet and found a notice about a married Anglican priest by the same name being received into the Roman Catholic priesthood in Scotland. Hmm . . . . J was Scottish. The brief summary of his career in the article didn't mention any time in New York—well no, I guess it wouldn't. And the article gave a different first name for his wife. I wondered if that was our J, and if his first marriage had been lost in the wreckage. But I did an image search. No. That Fr. J didn't look anything like our J.

D's fall was so public. So embarrassing. There was no way to pretend it hadn't happened. But the obvious shambles of his life provided an undeniable rock bottom from which his recovery could begin—if it hadn't, he would have just danced on until he had danced himself to death. The truth just about killed him, but it did set him free.

J? He disappeared. J was so gifted, in so many ways. I hope he is no longer dividing himself into separate compartments. I hope he is no longer juggling two selves, or more. One self is about all any of us can handle.

The priest who sold crack out of his rectory. The one who slept with the soprano in the choir. The rector who was too drunk by 9 a.m. on Sunday morning to celebrate the Eucharist. The one caught with pornography on his computer, and the one who molested children for decades. These send shock waves far and wide. People want us to be good. Some of them even want us to be good on their behalf! We take vows to be good examples. People apologize to us if they use a four-letter word in our presence, as if we didn't let a few choice ones fly ourselves when provoked. Publicly illumined for years by the rosy imaginings of other people, we fall mightily when we fall.

And we collude in their inflating of our goodness. We like being thought better than we are. Who would not? It may be that we are attracted to ministry partly *because* of the cracks we sense in our own goodness. *I will be safe from myself there. The honor accorded me will protect me. I won't act on my desires.* They think we're better than we are; we hide in the protective coloration of the high regard in which we are held. I don't suggest that this is a conscious decision on our part; rather, it is a means by which we hope to conceal our unlovelier truths, conceal them even from ourselves. No human enterprise is pure, and we are human beings, with both sunny and shady reasons for the things we do. Your call to ministry may be true and powerful, but it will always have a shadow side. Ignore the shadow, and it won't go away meekly. It will go underground.

Because the pedestal is higher than it should be, the fall from it is worse. The community is angry at having been betrayed, and now finds it difficult to find any good at all in the one exposed as a sinner. But this is as wrongheaded as lionizing us was—we are *all* more than our worst misdeed. The good that J did in so many settings was truly good. D was loved and depended upon in his parishes because he was lovable and did good work, even though for years he wasn't sober while he was doing it. Setting aside for a moment the probability that he would have done even better work if he hadn't been high most of the time, there was a reason why people adored him, and there was a reason why his rector took the unusual course of restoring him to his position after his stint in rehab. D was immensely good, and everyone knew it.

To whom can something like this happen? Who will crash and burn? Some are obvious time bombs and nobody is surprised when they explode. But this is not the case with most people. Most people are good and wish to *do* good. In most cases, the demons combine with the wrong place and wrong time to ensnare legitimate human desires and render them monstrous. All the good things in life—reputation, skill, money, love—call to all of us, and we reach eagerly back for them. Let something weaken us, and we can make an idol out of anything.

Alcoholics in recovery have an acronym for the warning signs that trouble might be ahead: it is HALT. It stands for HUNGRY, ANXIOUS, LONELY, TIRED. I have also heard that the "A" is for "angry." That works, too.

This acronym is eloquent—it says what it means. If something is bothering you, stop and pay attention to it. Find a sane way to make it better. If you're hungry, eat. Tired? Rest, for heaven's sake. Lonely? Reach out to someone. Anxious or angry? Acknowledge that this is so and that it might make you susceptible to the wrong kind of self-care. Talk out your anger with a colleague you trust—if you don't have one, view that fact as a danger sign (and be sure to read to the end of this chapter). Consult a psychotherapist—if you're in ministry, you should know the good ones in your community. If you don't, view that fact as another danger sign. If you don't think people of faith should consult secular therapists, grow up. We're in the twenty-first century now.

Face what is stressing you directly, with all the tools available to a modern person, and you will be less likely to try and fix it indirectly. Care for yourself in a good way or—most assuredly—you will care for yourself in a bad way.

If HALT has weakened you, anything can become your false god. Alcohol, for sure, if that is your disease, or some other drug. But shopping can become a false god, too, and so can food. So can computer solitaire—anything can become the thing to which you turn for comfort and familiarity, can become that thing you think of before you think of anything else, that thing to which you begin to turn whenever you have opportunity.

Your false god doesn't have to be a bad thing—it is more alluring to a person to whom ethics are important, in fact, if it is a good one. Thus, pastoral work is often the clergy drug of choice—who can disapprove of a priest who spends all her time at the church? Her parishioners are apt to admire her extraordinary devotion uncritically, since they benefit from it. Who will suspect that this has become a way of avoiding being home, when it is so irreproachable? "The last temptation is the greatest treason: to do the right deed for the wrong reason," wrote T. S. Eliot in *Murder in the Cathedral*, and it is true.

"I feel for my colleagues who are not in good spiritual shape," says Victoria, the concert organist-turned-priest. "I wish I could help them more. They don't all seem to understand the cosmic forces with which we are dealing constantly and the absolute necessity for being in good spiritual shape. It is so easy for our egos to get in the way and for ministry to seem like it is about getting ahead, obtaining more power, getting lots of people to come to church, balancing the books, and being in control. I don't think that is what concerned Jesus when he walked this earth."

No, it probably wasn't.

Charlie, Lisa, Bob, Blake, Troy, Bonnie, and me. We met once a month at Charlie's church, where coffee and donuts were always waiting when we arrived. When Charlie retired, we and the donuts moved to Bob's, and John and Carlye joined us. Bonnie died. Lisa moved to Pennsylvania. When Bob retired, we moved to John's church in Yonkers, where Helen joined us. The group was losing momentum by that point, and soon it folded quietly. Nothing lasts forever. But it was a lifesaver for a long time. Wayward children, difficult parishes, physical illnesses—we shared them all with each other. The first hour was spent talking together, maybe about a current topic or maybe just about what was going on in our world. In the second hour, we paired off, each pair finding a corner of the church building in which to practice very careful listening. Here is how it went: you talk for twenty minutes or so, and I listen to you carefully. I comment on what I have heard. Then we change places—I talk and you listen. At the end, the group comes together again for some closing prayer. That was how we did it, anyway.

Our rule was that two clergy from the same parish couldn't join the group—you'll probably need to complain about your parish sometimes, and you won't be free to do so with a colleague there. You might even need to complain about the colleague.

Our group was golden. We grew to love each other, and we told each other things we'd never told another living soul. Every clergyperson should have a group like this, and so should a lot of other people. Put one together before you need it because of some crisis in your life—we don't think very clearly at such times. It can save your sanity. Nobody really knows what it is to do this work except other people who do this work, not even the most devoted spouse. We are not free to share at this level with our parishioners—we have a fiduciary duty to them which they do not have toward us, and this kind of sharing requires a parity we cannot expect from the people committed to our charge.

How do you go about setting up such a group? Think of a few people you like and respect—you don't need to know them well already, but you should have a positive feeling about them. Ask more than you need: not everyone you invite will accept. Consider the geographical location of potential members, and only invite people for whom getting together once a month will be feasible—someone who must drive four hours to get to you should start a group of his own, with people who are near him. When you invite, choose a date and time for a first meeting at least a month from the day you invite—people are busy. Let potential members know that these could change, and that the group will decide about that together.

Have a plan for the gathering. Have a definite time frame—not longer than two hours. Start and finish on time—people are busy. Maybe you will do what our group did: a plenary time discussing a topic and then paired listening sessions. Or just stay together in plenary, have an individual check-in time in which each person talks about what's happening in his or her life, and then discuss a topic—if your group is small, this is probably the way to go. Just gathering for a chat without structure will make it harder for the introverts among you to have their say—the social butterflies will take over, and so will diocesan gossip. Some form of mutual invitation to everyone to speak and a format that everyone understands at the outset will give everyone a chance. Even if you have every confidence in the discretion of your colleagues, verbally assert the confidentiality of the group—*What is said here, stays here*. Every one of us has had the disconcerting experience of being told something we really ought not to know about someone who is not present. It is never a mistake to warn against such a thing.

If the group chooses to address a topic for the first hour of your meeting, what should it be? Go back to the basics of why you became a priest in the first place. You entered this life because you had a strong attraction to the things of God. You cared about prayer, about liturgy, about Scripture, about theology, about service to the world. Choose one of those things and talk about it for about an hour at each meeting.

In the years since your ordination, your approach to some of these things has changed—over a lifetime, we *evolve* in those things about which we care deeply. Life teaches and shapes us. We are not precisely the same people we were in our twenties, and we are not the same people now that we will be in twenty years. We understand the community of priests to be a *college,* a fellowship of people dedicated to one another, and talking together about those things that make us what we are is a powerful engine of our evolution.

How many people should be in your group? Eight at the most, I would say, so that plenary exchange is possible. Ideally, it will be an even number, so that people can pair off, if that's how you decide your group will work—but if it sometimes is not an even number because someone is missing, one pair can become a trio.

Consider where you will meet. Of course, you could rotate hosting duties among the members. We did not, and for a reason: in spiritual direction (and this is a form of it) setting is an important part of the encounter. Use the human capacity for operant conditioning to your advantage—meeting at the same place, at the same time, with the same people will trigger members' relaxed receptivity to the experience of community in a way that adjusting to a different setting every time you meet will not.

Ask people who intend to continue in the group to commit to it—not that there should be some kind of sanction against them if they miss a meeting, but ask them to make attending a serious priority. The more consistently people attend, the more you will care about each other and the more useful the group will be to everyone. Give the group time to bond—you won't be intimate after one meeting. After a year of meetings, you will be.

And there will be times when you will need that kind of intimacy.

Sometimes we find ourselves in the wrong place. *Did I make a mistake in coming to this church?* you ask yourself. That is a question everyone asks at times, no matter what they do for a living. Usually the answer is *No, not really.* You're just having a terrible day.

But sometimes the answer is *Yes, I'm afraid you did.* The discernment you and the parish did when you were called there seems not to have been well founded. They thought you were somebody you were not, and you thought they were something other than what they were. Maybe you wear glasses just like the ones your predecessor wore, or drive the exact same car, or you were a singer like he was, or you went to high school with a member of the search committee. That has nothing to do with it, you told each other and yourselves as you began to fall in love. Now you are not so sure. Was I thinking magically and not aware of it? Were we all doing that? Maybe—we never do realize it when we think magically. We never do see everything there is to see: we see what we want to be true. Both parties put their best foot forward. In the pink clouds of hope that surround a search process and a new ministry, you did not see each other clearly at first. Usually everyone figures out how to accommodate a more accurate picture of one another. Sometimes, though, they can't get there.

In an Episcopal parish, there used to be no gentle way to dissolve a pastoral relationship gone terribly wrong—a rector was firmly in place if he wanted to be there, unless he was caught stealing money, sleeping with the wrong person or publicly drunk. It is now canonically possible, with the help of the bishop and her staff, mutually to end something that cannot work—"gentle" is probably not the best word here, any more than a no-fault divorce could with any honesty be described as gentle, but it is at least possible. No one is happy: the congregation feels held back by a rector who cannot lead them in a way they can follow, and the rector faces precipitous loss of both salary and housing, which few clergy can afford. Yes, it's better than a witch hunt, but everyone is still scarred when it's over.

This could happen to you. It could happen to your favorite colleague. Search processes are full of safeguards intended to help us all not think magically, but we don't always internalize them, and some parishes ignore them. You will need your support group at a time like this. You will need them to encourage you. To help you not make the same mistake again, and—if they really love you—to help you see where your ego may have propelled you down the terrible path you just survived. If you're fortunate enough to have such sisters and brothers, you may hate hearing what they have to say. Listen especially to the parts you hate hearing the most. They're probably onto something.

Speaking of the desert, there's something else you probably ought to know: being a priest can get you killed.

Charlie apprehended the church sexton in the act of molesting a child in the parish kitchen. In the aftermath of the discovery, the man projected his own self-hatred upon Charlie. The man's wife threatened to leave him. Charlie remembers, "I began receiving disturbing phone calls from Eddie, sometimes in the middle of the night: 'Is Reverend Home-Wrecker there?' There were many voiceless calls in which he would stay on the line without saying a word, then hang up. Eddie's wife called one day to say, 'Eddie has taken our dining room furniture out into the backyard and has begun chopping it up with an ax, saying he is cutting you up in little pieces.' A few weeks later, she called again to say that she thought that Eddie was on his way down to St. Barnabas with a gun and that he was coming after me. . . ." All this happened years ago. Not long after these events, Eddie suffered a stroke which completely disabled him. He was no longer a threat.

But still, Charlie says, "Even today, I will not put my back to my office window at night."

This is not at all an unusual occurrence. There are unbalanced people in this world, and the profound deficit in personal power with which they live daily often makes them seek out churches—many church people are welcoming and kind. The clergy are trained to be good listeners. It is easy for the wounded to find a place in the house of God, and church people are usually not aware at first of the depth of the newcomer's illness. Most of the urban clergy I know have been threatened with violence at least once, some more than once. I myself have been stalked twice, the second time by a man who was later connected through DNA with at least six rapes. He called the bishop's office to say that I would be murdered in three days, and the police got him right outside the church before the three days were up. I got a knife away from another man who pulled it on me in our chapel—he ran away, weaponless. I kept that knife as a reminder that tomorrow is promised to none of us. I was knocked to the ground in the hallway outside the church office by an angry drunk—he and I went off in separate ambulances, he to Bellevue and I to the nearest emergency room, where they sewed up a cut on my elbow.

So we don't always land in the desert on our own. Sometimes the desert seeks us out. I suppose some of these things could have been avoided, but I for one was never willing to seal myself off from the world to the extent that would have been required to ensure my safety against all comers. That's just no way for a priest to live—or anybody else, come to think of it.

Nobody is completely safe. As my friend Orrie used to say, none of us are getting out of here alive.

## BATTER MY HEART,
## THREE-PERSON'D GOD

Batter my heart, three-person'd God, for you
As yet but knock, breathe, shine, and
   seek to mend;
That I may rise and stand, o'erthrow me,
   and bend
Your force to break, blow, burn,
   and make me new.
I, like an usurp'd town to another due,
Labor to admit you, but oh, to no end;
Reason, your viceroy in me, me should defend,
But is captiv'd, and proves weak or untrue.
Yet dearly I love you, and would be
   lov'd fain,
But am betroth'd unto your enemy;
Divorce me, untie or break that knot again,
Take me to you, imprison me, for I,
Except you enthrall me, never shall be free,
Nor ever chaste, except you ravish me.

John Donne, 1618

# 3
# THE DANCE OF THE PRIEST

**NO MATTER HOW GOOD YOU WERE** in school, it takes some time to get good at ministry. But time passes and you work hard. You learn from your mentors and learn even more from your mistakes. The fits and starts of your formation—things you thought you'd be good at and weren't, things you never imagined doing well that turned out to be some of your strong points—these revelations are behind you now. The straight shots and the blind alleys of your early years—all these are history now, too. You have some mileage now. There are now many people newer at this than you are.

You must appear at the hospital in the middle of the night because a parishioner has been killed in a car crash.

You must wade into the wreckage of a family hurtling toward divorce.

You must comfort parents who have just lost a child.

You must be present when a patient receives a bleak prognosis.

You must receive the anger of a parishioner who is leaving and wants to tell you about it.

You must accompany sorrow and despair.

You now know how to do all these things. You know that you are not magic. That you cannot make things go away. That the burdens people bear are their own. But you know how to be there in a way that helps them.

Now your work is like a dance whose steps you know. Not the kind in which you just shift from foot to foot and wave your arms out on the dance floor all by yourself, but an intricate dance, a dance that depends on other people. A dance whose beauty lies in the whole company, not just in your solo. A square dance, maybe.

Trinity Church, Wall Street. The richest church in the world, if you don't count the Vatican, which isn't exactly a church. Trinity's cemetery is filled with the great and the near great of Episcopal New York history and New York history in general; marble plaques sacred to the memory of their largesse adorn the walls. J. P. Morgan was a member of Trinity, and so was Alexander Hamilton. George Washington went to church at its nearby chapel on the day of his inauguration. Trinity used to own all of lower Manhattan, and it has made wise use of its great wealth.

The rector in my day was originally from New Hampshire, but he was raised in Tennessee and had served several churches in the South before coming to Trinity in the late 1980s. He was a famous preacher. Though many might think they can, the number of people who actually *could* run a place like Trinity is pretty small—it's a big ship to steer. It is also a place that values elegance and a certain corporate decorum, and sets a high bar for it. Which is why members of the senior staff were taken aback one day when, at a planning meeting for a series of conferences Trinity was planning for several locations around the country, the rector told them all to get out of their chairs and move everything—chairs and even the large conference table—to the perimeter of the room. They were going to square dance. It turned out that Dan is a square dance caller, and a good one. Tennessee, you know.

PROMENADE YOUR PARTNER . . .

GRAB THAT NEIGHBOR COUPLE

AND CIRCLE UP FOUR . . .

SWING THAT OUTSIDE LADY . . .

AND NOW YER SUGAR BABE . . .

Men in wing tips and women in black pumps moved uncertainly through the calls.

RIGHT HANDS OVER AND HOWDY DO . . .

LEFT HAND BACK AND HOW ARE YOU?

The dancers clasped right and then left hands briefly as they moved past one another—this seemed more complex than it really was to most of them. But some of them were gaining confidence enough to help the others, though there was scarcely time to do more than grab a stray's shoulder and spin him around so the other dancers wouldn't run him over.

YER GOIN' THE WRONG WAY!

There were a few panicked looks among the dancers, but this criticism was not to be taken personally or professionally—it was just a signal to reverse direction in the dance. Back they all went, to the left this time.

This memory doesn't sting like the one of the man at

the gas station, but I have never forgotten it, either—what we learned square dancing was more than one would think. The dance was an allegory. You don't accomplish anything successfully all by yourself. Everything that works does so because a team does it. Anything you do well alone, you will do better in community. The sooner you come to understand this and practice it, the better. We don't have to be amazing people—very few of us are amazing. But we can fit together in amazing ways, and the sum of us is what makes a community amazing.

This is the dance. You know who you are and what you do best. You know how to help other people do the same.

A friend of mine used to think of herself as being rather like an old-fashioned telephone switchboard operator: connecting people to each other over the most direct line available, plugging people into the places from which they could do what they did best. We had been talking about how to get it all done in a parish and agreeing that it was fairly impossible. But I can still see her gesture—reaching up to pull an imaginary plug from where it was and placing it into an imaginary slot somewhere else on the imaginary board. Just about every need she was filling was something she could easily have done herself, and some of them were things she might have enjoyed doing. But there was only one of her. And she wasn't there to do everything: she was there to see that everything got done. A priest doesn't just do God's work—God's work is something everybody must find a way to do. What the priest does is gather the *people* to do God's work.

Though we were both new priests, I was much younger than my friend when we had this conversation. I was still doing what young people must do: gathering my powers, assembling and polishing the tools that I would use to become the priest I would become. I recall being a little disappointed as she spoke—you mean I won't get to do all these cool things myself? Maybe not even the ones I'd be really good at? My ministry really is about enabling *other* people? Would I ever be as selfless as she seemed to be, and be that way so easily? The ego is large and a little unruly in young leaders, and it's entirely appropriate that it be so—we are constructing ourselves. Moreover, we have just completed an educational process in which the focus was entirely on us and the skills we were developing. We can be forgiven for thinking at first that we are the stars of our own ministries.

Some people never move beyond that conviction. Most of us do, with occasional relapses into its alluring but useless embrace. Free yourself as soon as you can. As a priest, you're not going for Best Actress—you want Best Supporting Actress. Each time I've forgotten that, whatever movie I thought I was making at the time hasn't been a very good one. Remembering it requires some vigilance, some consistent way of reminding yourself that *none* of it is all about you. Not even your sermon, when you're standing in the pulpit all alone and everyone is watching only you and listening to only you—even *that* moment is not primarily about you. It's not even *mostly* about you, not even if the sermon you're preaching uses *biographical material from your own life*. Nope—if it's not also about them, if there is no ready way for those listening to connect your experience with theirs, you have sunk like a stone.

Ministry is a paradox: it is only if you cultivate the ability to forget yourself that you can serve effectively. This has equivalents in other professions: for a dancer, it is "Don't look at your feet." For a pianist, it is "Don't look at your hands." You must learn how effectiveness feels in *integration* with your task, which you can't do if your focus is on yourself rather than on the task at hand and the people you serve. You learn to minister by ministering. In time, the duty you have to others becomes so much a part of you that you stop looking in the mirror. You learn to take your cues and gauge your effectiveness by what is happening around you, not just inside you. Within and among the people committed to your charge, not just within you. I have known priests who believed it was sufficient for a leader just to be genuinely himself. Though authenticity is necessary, it is by no means sufficient, and it is dangerous to suppose otherwise—*Hitler* was genuinely himself. I have no reality check if my only barometer is my inner voice.

Fr. Mychal Judge, the Franciscan priest who was chaplain to the New York City Fire Department until his death at the World Trade Center in 2001, often used this prayer: *Lord, take me where you want me to go, let me meet who you want me to meet, tell me what you want me to say, and keep me out of your way.* Mychal didn't think God led him around like a puppet on a string—what he was praying for was his own continual need to confine himself to the task at hand and to trust that the power that had brought him thus far wouldn't desert him now.

Don't look at your feet. Don't look at your hands. And don't worry about what your next step might mean for your career. We don't *have* careers while we're serving—we just have a chance to do something worth doing today, and then a chance to do another one tomorrow, and the next day, and the next. The next right thing is the only thing we ever need to do. You don't do a whole square dance all at once; you do it step by step. "Getting in God's way" is the train wreck that happens to us when we lose sight of this.

The power that created the universe courses through you when you've learned to allow it, like electricity through a wire. This doesn't mean that every choice you make will be the right one or that everything for which you pray will happen as you hope it will. Certainly not: Mychal Judge *died* guided by his prayer about not getting in God's way. But it does mean that you find yourself doing things you were pretty sure you could not do, as was just as certainly true of Mychal. Once I've done the best I can with what I have at hand, I must turn it over. There are more important things in the world than my own survival, many of them, and larger forces at work in the world than my own strength. Not everything I do will succeed. But everything will matter.

Who will separate us from the love of Christ?
Will hardship, or distress, or persecution, or
famine, or nakedness, or peril, or sword? As it
is written, "For your sake we are being killed
all day long; we are accounted as sheep to be
slaughtered." No, in all these things we are
more than conquerors through him who loved
us. For I am convinced that neither death, nor
life, nor angels, nor rulers, nor things present,
nor things to come, nor powers, nor height, nor
depth, nor anything else in all creation, will
be able to separate us from the love of God in
Christ Jesus our Lord.

Romans 8:35–39

In the square dance, everyone matters. The compli-
cated patterns—and even the simple ones—depend upon
everyone knowing what to do and doing it, knowing where
to be and being there. The loveliness of it is the community
it creates, a community always in motion, moving out and
in, around and over, to the right and to the left, but always
together, intricate in its kaleidoscopic beauty.

Many dance forms in Asia are closely related to story
telling, like the Kathakali dancers of the Kerala region
in southern India, with their enormous skirts, elaborate
makeup, their towering headdresses. Or the many different
styles of dance in Thailand, each one with a specific purpose in communal life: preparation for battle, courtship,

preparation for a wedding, celebration of a community, celebration of the harvest, friendly but earnest competition with another town. Though they may not all be what a Westerner might call religious in nature, they are certainly liturgical, with traditional rules of performance and costume—and even facial expression—that go back centuries.

In 1970s Cambodia, the Pol Pot regime murdered 1.5 million Cambodians, one-fifth of the total population. The regime targeted intellectuals, property owners, business leaders. It also targeted artists—only one in ten Cambodian artists lived through it. Those who survived the Khmer Rouge did so by concealing the fact of their vocation and training. The ancient artistic and intellectual traditions of Cambodia were almost completely wiped out. Musical instruments were confiscated and destroyed. The dancers' intricately constructed costumes and headdresses, some centuries old, were discarded as useless rags. There were now dances nobody living knew how to perform anymore. The Khmer Rouge understood well the power of the dance. If their art could be erased, the people would cease to exist as a people. They would become whatever the regime told them they were.

The years since the fall of that bloody regime have seen a feverish effort to restore what was lost. Teachers whose bodies had been ruined in the backbreaking work of the fields worked with expatriate dancers and musicians who had fled and had now returned, to study the old forms and recapture them in a movement to redeem the unspeakable losses of a terrible time. In the decades since then, the music and the dances have returned, passed down from the few who knew them to a few and then to a few more young people. For them, it is all new. They remember neither the old ways nor the killing fields of the Khmer Rouge. The ancient beauty of the dance itself is what draws them.

One of the best things about the dance is the opportunity to help other people learn how to do it. The more peopled it is with partners, the more beautiful the dance becomes. Mentoring newcomers to ministry has been built into the church since it was new. For several centuries and in my early years, this usually happened in the relationship between rector and curate, an experienced priest taking a new one under his or her wing for a few years. The relationship is not primarily an educational one—the curate is no longer a student. She is more like an resident in medicine: already a physician, but practicing under supervision for a time, refining her craft and gaining confidence. That's what a curate does, before the responsibility of being at the helm descends fully upon her. It was a good way to train.

I say *was*. The number of curacies in the Episcopal Church has declined significantly, and with them the chance to make some early mistakes while there is somebody close at hand to help you catch them. Only very large and wealthy parishes can afford curates today. Now, newly ordained people are likely to find themselves in charge of small parishes right out of seminary, with the support of an experienced priest in a nearby parish. That support may be more nominal than actual.

Church people uniformly decry this development, seeing in it yet another indicator of the church's decline and fall. I doubt it. It's just a change. Certainly becoming the vicar of a church right out of seminary is a lot like being tossed into the deep end of a swimming pool—and anybody who thinks pastoring a small church is easier than pastoring a large one has never done it. But one thing small parishes have that large ones lack is the awareness of their own need for everyone to lend a hand. The only ordained leader of a small church has no choice but to rely heavily on the gifts of the members of his congregation. She knows immediately when she has overestimated their capability and desire, or her own. A large paid staff can insulate a leader from this important information and breed passivity in the membership, who know that the jobs that need doing will get done without any help from them. It can be hard for them to feel that their presence makes a difference. If the challenge of a small parish is the discouraging search for new ways to get blood from a stone, that of a large one is the pleasant-tasting poison of complacency.

Besides, the parish structure with which we are familiar—a local congregation worshipping in its own building led by professional clergy—is probably on its way out, at least as the basic unit of ministry. There will always be an appetite for reverent liturgy, for seriously fine music and excellent preaching in a beautiful and historic architectural setting. But we will no longer consider this a normative standard in every place; there will be, and already are, many arenas for sharing the Good News and participation in the life of Christ in ways that speak to many different kinds of people, from virtual communities to small house churches to new models of monastic life to structures that do not yet exist, not even in our imaginations. The same will be true of the diocesan, national, and international structures we now know. We will adjust—we are adjusting right now—to a world that views centralized institutions of any kind with indifference, if not with outright suspicion. The considerable project of superimposing medieval hierarchy upon an egalitarian society will topple under its own weight, and the energy needed to sustain it will migrate to other forms of service.

Paradoxically, the same virtual opportunities for community that promised an enhanced presence of traditional church structures in the world also threaten their existence. Initially, the online presence of a forward-looking parish was intended to make people want to come to church services and participate in parish activities. *Come this Sunday and hear a good sermon, some beautiful music.* Now the virtual component of parish life stands alone with ease, many people tuning into it from a distance, reading clergy blogs at computer terminals far away from the church building, reading them at any time convenient, not just at 11 a.m. on a Sunday morning. What can make a parish's reach wide can also make it narrow—I need never meet anyone in the parish face-to-face. I may never visit the church building itself. I can get everything on my computer, here at home. I can hear the sermon from one place, the music from another. There is no particular reason for me to affiliate with either one. There is, in fact, no reason for me to affiliate with *anyone*.

Church people also view *this* development with alarm—you probably noticed long ago that we view most new things with alarm. For the generation that did not grow up with computers, it seems a pale image of personal contact, too diffuse to do any lasting good. It seems to endorse and appropriate the general culture's consumerist approach to everything we encounter, inquiring no further than the lowest-hanging fruit, no further than the first answer to the question *What's in it for me?*

In particular, it is the sacrifice of the Eucharist which seems least transferable to a virtual experience of church. The physical intimacy of the common cup, the broken bread, the physicality of the act of kneeling, of standing—watching these things is not the same as doing them.

But still—I remember a remarkable experience of the Eucharist during the consecration of a bishop, which was happening in a city forty miles from the parish. The cathedral couldn't possibly have held the thousands of people who wished to attend. But it would stream the service live, and we were encouraged to watch it together in our parishes. Twenty of us gathered in the Fryer Room, where our video projector was set up. True, the procession was unimpressive on the small screen. We did not kneel or stand. We did not sing; we listened. I'm afraid I do not recall the sermon—never a good sign. But when it came time for the communion, something changed. I set out the elements on the coffee table: bread and wine in the silver vessels on a snowy white corporal. I made the manual acts while the celebrant spoke the words, touching the chalice and the bread as *she* did, signing them with a cross as *she* did, lifting them as *she* did, breaking the bread as *she* did. Then we passed the body and blood of Christ to one another—the room was too crowded to do it in the normal way, so the chalice and paten simply went from hand to hand, from person to person. At the end we sat quietly and watched the procession wind its way out of the cathedral.

Had there been no communion there in the Fryer Room, had we only watched, we would have spent that hour and a bit more simply watching television. The physicality of our local celebration, though, blended with what was happening on the screen. The two met and brought the entire experience into our hearts. Watching people come and go for communion in the cathedral, we were there with them. Here and there on the screen, we glimpsed a familiar face— there was Phil Carr-Jones, there was Anne LeMay, there was Ed Zelley. Christ lovingly spanned the miles between us and them, through the medium of the Internet.

I realized, also, that it would not have been necessary for me to have been there. This was a celebration of the Eucharist that could have happened in a parish without a priest present—a layperson could have performed the actions I performed, while the bishop spoke the words. In the Episcopal Church, it's important that a priest say the words that transform ordinary bread and wine into the body and blood of Christ, and one did. She and we were just not in the same physical space. But Christ is not in the same physical space we occupy, either, yet he is present.

What the Internet can provide is a glimpse for earth-bound souls of what the domain of God is like. The simultaneity of heaven, in which there is no time and no physical separation, is hard for us to grasp until we begin to reflect upon what virtual reality is like. There, too, our experience of events is not locked into one time slot or imprisoned in one place. People *do* need one another's physical presence. Sitting in your bedroom staring at a screen will not satisfy for long. Though we can still say we would like to have been there when the bishop was consecrated, we recall that we couldn't have been there anyway—there wasn't room in the cathedral. So we experienced it where we were. It is possible to share the experiences of faith combining the virtual and actual ways, to the enhancement of both. Distance did not defeat us. Virtual reality did for us what the first Eucharist did for the first Christians—it gave them the experience of Christ long after the historical Jesus was no longer among them.

So, in a sense, the Eucharist itself, as we understand it, is a form of virtual reality.

4

# THE DEATH OF THE PRIEST

**I WAS IN THE SHOWER WHEN** the phone rang, so Q took the call. It was Brother Clark. It was hard, even then, for Q to keep track of people's names and locations in our life, and I could tell when I emerged, wrapped in a towel, that he couldn't place who Brother Clark was, nor did he recall knowing Brother Justus. So he was taken aback at my profound reaction to the message he took: Justus is dead.

"What did you say?"

"Someone who comes to see you has died. Brother Justus."

"Justus?!? Are you saying Justus is dead?"

I asked him to repeat it several times, as one does when news is too terrible to take in. Through the fog of my disbelief, I couldn't seem to make Q understand that this was not just a regrettable bit of news about the death of an acquaintance. It was more than that, much more: Justus was my right hand. We worked together for years—he was my assistant in the office at Trinity, my colleague at the hospital and in the bag lunch program and in the men's shelter at St. Paul's Chapel. He was my deacon at the seaport, my lighting designer in the theater, my friend, my friend, my friend. Most of all, Justus was my friend.

I reached Clark on the phone.

Justus had been serving in Papua, New Guinea, where

the Franciscans have a friary. He was also the principal of the theological college there. There was much to do. The brothers there were in need of more formation in monastic community than they had been given theretofore, and the college needed strengthening as well, in many ways: its curriculum, its faculty, its buildings. The long hours and hard work seemed to agree with Justus, though: the last time we saw each other, he looked different from the way he looked when we served together years before—he was lean and muscular now, his pale skin burnished by the tropical sun in which he spent his days. He looked healthier and stronger than I'd ever seen him. How could he be dead?

He had caught a cold. That was no reason not to take a group of students camping in the mountains after their term at the college was over, as they had been planning. Papua New Guinea is remote anyway, and the trek up the mountain took them even farther away from human habitations. His cold grew worse after a few days, and it settled in his lungs. Soon, he could tell that he had developed pneumonia. The campers started back down toward the nearest village, a long journey over rough terrain. He grew worse, and soon he could no longer walk or even stand. The students lashed together a traverse for him to lie on, and they continued their desperate journey back down to civilization, dragging him along behind them over the bumpy ground.

They did not reach the village in time. They were less than a mile away, but it was too late.

Weeping, the young men clustered around their teacher as he struggled to speak.

*Don't think that you have failed because we didn't make it to the clinic. My ministry here is ended now. I'm going to continue my ministry with Christ, and you will stay here to carry on our work in the world.*

And Justus was gone. I preached at one of his funerals—he had several, in different parts of the world. I don't remember what I said. Even now, as I recount this story a decade after his death, I can't believe he's really gone. It still feels as though he were just away on one of his extended tours of duty. It feels as though he will be back. I think of him in pictures: Justus, coming out of his office at Trinity with a sheaf of papers in his hand. Justus, wheeling a cart overflowing with bag lunches up to St. Paul's chapel. Justus in a hard hat, covered with Ground Zero dust. Justus and me, one frigid Christmas Eve, celebrating the Eucharist on a picket line with striking *Daily News* workers—we used a battered tin cup and plate that he brought from home.

Still, today, they come: In a cathedral procession, he carries the Gospel book on his right shoulder. At Goldwater Hospital, he pushes a patient on a gurney into the chapel for the Sunday Eucharist. On Good Friday, we carry a large wooden cross he made throughout Lower Manhattan, and he settles it gently on the shoulders of an old woman who begs to be allowed to carry it just a little way: The Cross is Laid on Simon of Cyrene. And on a chilly Easter morning, we share Eucharist as the sun comes up over the East River.

Justus was my lighting director for a number of shows. A memory: An actress delivers a funny monologue, but her last and best line consistently fails to get a laugh. So Justus cuts out her spotlight as soon as she has spoken the line—and, night after night, the audience erupts in laughter. And when Thomas Becket is murdered in front of the altar at St. John's in the Village, Justus waits a horrified second and then gives us the flashing blue and red lights of a police squad car. As a director, I am often vague in my requests for the effect I want. Justus listens to me carefully and then goes up to the balcony to tinker with lighting equipment long past its prime. Time after time, he gives me perfection.

New Year's Day at St. Elizabeth's Friary in Flatbush, long before anybody in New York was talking about Flatbush becoming the next hot neighborhood: Brothers and parishioners, down-on-their-luck houseguests, neighborhood children and their parents sit down to a wonderful meal the brothers have prepared. After dinner, as afternoon turns to evening, we have Vespers in the chapel. Happy New Year.

Which tense to use now, in speaking and thinking of him? Is Justus a *was*, or an *is*? Oh, that's easy: he is both. Justus is in Christ, who was and is and is to come. He is all around me, all around us—and he sends me memory after memory, and each memory makes me more grateful that he is in my life. He is closer to me than he was before he died. They all are.

People die as they live. I think Tolstoy said that. It was true in this case—Justus was self-aware and self-giving. His greatest joy was serving. His thoughts were for his students, right to the end. With what little strength he had left, he wanted to leave them something that would help them in the days to come, and he did. "Do what you are doing," the Benedictines say, which means to give your full attention to the moment you are in. Justus was doing that in the very moment of his death.

What we hope is that our lives will be complete. By "complete," we *think* we mean "long." But these two words are not synonyms. There will always be unfinished business—the unreturned library books, the moving boxes still not unpacked, the unanswered letters, the prescriptions still at the drugstore. Maybe you should delete that plaintive e-mail from an old lover that you were holding on to for no good reason.

But it is not its brevity or its unfinished business that make a life incomplete. It is not even being cut far too short—dying in childhood, for instance, or young adulthood, although it is impossible for a grieving mother or father or spouse to think otherwise. But consider: We do not value a ten-year-old because she may someday be an astrophysicist. We don't love her for the sake of what she will become. We love her for what she is *right now*. She will never be forty-three, but she was perfectly ten years old. It is the little girl we miss, more than the woman she would have become, even if we never stop wondering who, exactly, that woman would have been. When we spend some time—years, probably decades—turning this idea over and over through sleepless nights, we begin to sense some truth in it. She was complete in herself, right then and there. Yes, I wanted much more than I got, but I had her while I had her, and she was everything at that moment that she could possibly have been.

Justus was too young to die, we all thought. He was fifty-eight. He would have made excellent use of another thirty years. But Justus was complete. He had held nothing back. Everything he had, he used—every moment, every talent, every idea, every feeling, every experience. He was in his life with both feet. Money is not the only thing you can't take with you: You can't take experiences or memories or ideas or words or even love with you, not as we know any of these things. You have to spend them here. These currencies are only good here.

My grandparents brought their four boys to America from England early in the last century. They came first to Winnipeg and then across the border into North Dakota, where he served three tiny churches in three tiny prairie towns. I have often wondered why they came. I have some old photographs of their extended family at home, and they look prosperous enough—poverty did not drive him here. I suppose it was a sense of mission and new possibility. I never knew him, so I cannot speak to his sense of adventure.

It was bleak on the prairie. Somewhere I have a photograph of their house—not a tree in sight. The wind whipped at the paint year after year, wearing it away—everything in the town was gray. The skulls of nineteenth-century cattle still lay here and there at the side of the road, bleached by the sun right where the animals had fallen on a long-ago drive. Tumbleweed rolled for miles along the flat fields, unimpeded by any topographical features worth noting. For a few weeks a year, the terrain was green and studded with wild flowers, but not for long. For most of the year, it was brown and gray.

I have their account ledger, a long narrow book bound in leather. In it, I see that my grandfather was often paid in kind: oats for the horse, coal for the furnace, eggs, chickens. I see that my grandmother gave music lessons—even I remember that she was a fine pianist. She noted each payment she received in the account book: a nickel per lesson.

I have a photograph of the two of them in one of the little churches. It is Thanksgiving, I think—there is an arrangement of pumpkins and gourds in front of the altar, and the pulpit has been made into a corn shock, tall stalks of corn surrounding it, while another pile of fruits and vegetables decorates the lectern. A garland of leaves and vines starts at the lectern, reaches up to the crossing and back down to the pulpit. My grandmother stands at the lectern, her long hair in the style I remember her wearing decades later: one long braid, circling her head like a coronet. Her dress is one of the vague-looking sacques fashionable at the time. He is in the pulpit, looking like any other clergyman of that day or this one, for that matter—dark suit, Anglican collar. Both are smiling broadly.

"You ladies have outdone yourselves this year," they are saying. "This church has never looked better!"

That was kind. They were kind people. Truth to tell, the church looked like hell. It looked like somebody had overturned a fruit stand in that church. But they were the encouragers of their flock, and the ladies *had* worked hard. The church looked as good as it was going to look, and they deserved some praise.

Besides, somebody was taking their photograph! Nobody was pointing and shooting a lightweight camera casually in those days: a photograph meant that somebody stood for a long time behind a tripod, with a dark fabric shade over his head. Photography was serious business.

Times were hard, and it was a hard life. My grandfather collapsed on a train station platform, coming home from a church event: a massive heart attack, which he would not survive for long. They got him home, though, and he lived long enough for my father to get there by train from the East Coast to stand by his father's deathbed.

They were keeping the watch families keep at the end, watching the breath as it tries to continue and then concedes defeat, counting the lengthening seconds in between inhalations. Three, five, five, then seven, seven, seven—the last one is always something of a surprise to those keeping vigil, who do not know at first that it *was* the last one. But seven, then eight, nine, ten, eleven. Wait—is he gone?

Almost. My grandfather sat up, his blue eyes blazing as they looked straight ahead at something no one else could see. "I always knew you would come for me," he said, and fell back on the pillow, dead. My grandfather had lived his life in the expectation that Jesus would come for him when he died, and he did.

I never sat on his lap. I have no pet name by which I remember him, no name by which I called him, like "Granddad" or "Papa." How could I? He and I never met. I have few stories of him—my father seldom spoke of his childhood. But I have this story, and it is enough for me. My grandfather's was a life of service, and it was a hard life. But it was also a life of hope and trust, and he needed to hope and trust. We all do.

I recall theological conversations with leftist friends in the late 1960s, centering around the hope of heaven. It seemed to them—and looking back now, probably to me as well—that heaven was a fraudulent prize dangled in front of oppressed people to keep them quiet. I remember African American students my age who were dismissive of the Negro spirituals they had been raised with in church—what were these, but counsels to tolerate injustice? Oh, we were rock-hard in our youth, much harder than I am now in the autumn of my life. We were in love with our own untried righteousness, most admiring of our invincible fury. We could not imagine courage taking any form besides the frontal confrontation that shook those years, so we completely missed the courage it can take simply to endure.

I still know people who won't let themselves hope for heaven, who can't shake the feeling that doing so is in some way a craven acquiescence in the injustice of a harsh world. I am not one of them, though my hope is not in an anthropomorphic reiteration of the life we already know. There is a timeless mystery that surrounds and contains the mystery we are in now, and ours yields gratefully to it. In no way does this mean we have no responsibility for what the rabbis call the *tikkun*, the "repair of the world." It only permits us to accept without despair the limits of our power in this project, once we have pushed limits as far they can go. Brother Justus went as far as he could here. Then he told his grief-stricken students that his ministry was continuing with Christ. It may have been finished here. But it was not finished there.

## FELIX RANDAL

Felix Randal the farrier, O he is dead then?
  my duty all ended,
Who have watched his mould of man, big-boned
  and hardy-handsome
Pining, pining, till time when reason rambled
  in it and some
Fatal four disorders, fleshed there, all contended?

Sickness broke him. Impatient he cursed at first,
  but mended
Being anointed and all; though a heavenlier
  heart began some

Months earlier, since I had our sweet reprieve
    and ransom
Tendered to him. Ah well, God rest him all
    road ever he offended!

This seeing the sick endears them to us, us too
    it endears.
My tongue had taught thee comfort, touch had
    quenched thy tears,
Thy tears that touched my heart, child, Felix,
    poor Felix Randal;

How far from then forethought of, all thy more
    boisterous years,
When thou at the random grim forge, powerful
    amidst peers,
Didst fettle for the great grey drayhorse his
    bright and battering sandal!

                Gerard Manley Hopkins, 1918

Reading this poem, it will help to remember that Hopkins was a Roman Catholic priest, and that a farrier is a blacksmith. The "bright and battering sandal" in the last line is a horseshoe. The "reprieve and ransom" he tendered to Felix Randal was the body and blood of Christ in Holy Communion. No, this poem isn't about the death of a priest—it is about a priest attending a man to his death, and the sorrow of illness and of the good-bye.

PART TWO

# A PATH FORMED BY WALKING

# 1

# WRITER

## YOU LEARN TO WRITE BY READING.

Read everything you can get your hands on. Read good books and bad books, until you learn to tell the difference—in time, the bad ones will bore you. If a book is a classic and you can't for the life of you see why, ask somebody who already loves it. And don't just read useful books about your profession—good Lord, no. Read fiction. Read biography. Read history. Read the newspaper every day. Read the labels on cereal boxes, if there's nothing else at hand.

We learn to write by becoming used to seeing the words lie down on a page. We learn to hear in our minds what we read. We learn to form mental pictures of what we read, and we learn to love them. We are fiercely protective of our favorite literary characters. We pour narrow-minded scorn upon film versions in which characters don't look as we have imagined them.

Learn the grammar of our language. Know the rules, even if you decide in certain places not to follow them. Learn the ways of the apostrophe and use it correctly—no editor will want to read your stuff if you can't do that, and anyway, it's not rocket science. Your choice not to follow a grammatical rule should never look like a mistake—if it looks like a mistake, it *is* one. You might choose to use a sentence fragment instead of a complete sentence for a reason, but it can't be because you didn't know how to assemble a sentence properly.

Listen carefully to the ways in which people talk. People in real life don't speak precisely, the way they do in textbooks. They repeat themselves, grope for words, speak in fragments. If you can write dialogue intelligibly and still make it sound like people actually sound when they speak, you've got something going. Write every day, even if it's only one sentence. Writing every day primes the pump: writing makes you write. I know that this is hard for people who have a full-time job; I did it for years. Most writers do it for years, unless they were born into wealth. Hint: The easiest way to find the time to write every day is to stop watching television.

Never throw away anything you have written. Never. You may be able to use it someday. Now that we have computers, never throwing anything away doesn't have to mean that your house will be cluttered with your unfinished short stories. But if the God of Cancellation should happen to smile on you sometime when you're not near your computer and you find yourself with an unexpected half hour, find an old envelope and write on the back of that. You can transcribe later.

Do not wait until you can afford a new computer.

Do not wait until you retire.

Do not wait until you change jobs.

Do not wait until the children are grown.

Do not wait until tomorrow. You may be dead tomorrow.

And do not wait for inspiration. People imagine inspiration to be like a romantic movie about nineteenth-century writers who starve in Parisian garrets. Never ask yourself if you're feeling "inspired." What does that even mean? I don't believe in "inspiration." I believe in work. What is your inspiration? Your inspiration is that you've decided to write a book. Your inspiration is that you have a deadline. What your inspiration is *not* is a feeling that carries you ecstatically away. You don't need to be carried away. You just need to sit down and write.

Oh, and never use the word "incredibly." It weakens whatever word follows it. You can do better.

Thus far, this piece on a writer's vocation is an odd fit in a book about being *called* to things. All I've done in it so far is bark orders and give advice. Isn't there something to say about a writer's *call*? About the gift of writing itself? There must be such a thing as a gift, for a person could follow all my advice and still not turn out publishable work. Their work could be grammatically perfect and still not sing. They could have an iron writing discipline and, in the end, have nothing to show for it that anyone would want to read. This is the secret nightmare of every artist: *My stuff will be terrible, and nobody will want it.*

Nobody will read my work.

Nobody will come to my show.

Nobody will buy my paintings.

My ceramics.

My design.

My jewelry.

My needlework.

Nobody will want me.

Nobody will want me. No, it's not really *me*—it's only my short story. But our creative work is so much an extension of ourselves that it is hard for us not to take rejection of it personally. We must *learn* how not to do that; it doesn't come naturally to most of us. An actor friend just says "I wasn't right for the part" and moves on; nobody but him knows the number of blows to his ego that brought him to this philosophical attitude toward rejection.

The seventeenth-century poet John Milton published his own collected poems in 1645. They included every poem he had ever written up to that time, including some written when he was very young, poems he knew weren't very good. To my knowledge, he was the first person to have done that, and I'm not sure anybody has knowingly done it since. It's scary enough to publish work you think is good under your own name. I can't imagine putting out the other stuff. I would never have had the guts. Putting stuff out there takes guts.

There is a long history in literature of pseudonymous publication, writers publishing work under names other than their own. Jane Austen's first published book, for instance, was by "A Lady," and the next one was by "The Author of Sense and Sensibility." Although three more books would appear during her lifetime, none of them were published under her own name. The last two of her books published came out after her death, and only then did her name appear on the title page.

Ben Franklin had at least nine pen names: He was Silence Dogood, Caelia Shortface, Martha Careful, Busy Body, Anthony Afterwit, Alice Addertongue, Polly Baker, Benevolus, and, most famously, Richard Saunders, the author of *Poor Richard's Almanac*.

Molière, Voltaire, Woody Allen, Pablo Neruda, George Orwell, and Ayn Rand are all pen names.

What's in a pen name? Jane Austen, although she wrote at a time when there were some well-known female novelists and poets, lived a very private life in a rural setting. Perhaps some of her satiric characters came a bit too close in their resemblance to actual citizens of Steventon or Chawton for her to feel entirely comfortable with her name attached to the novels in which they appeared. We know it was not to disguise her gender; "a lady" is definitely a female. Sometimes people choose a pen name because it sounds more romantic or more cosmopolitan than their given name. Sometimes they use one to establish a different genre from the one for whom they have an audience—say, if a historian wanted to write a romance novel. Often it serves to disguise an ethnicity—Woody Allen's given name was Allen Stewart Konigsberg, which he changed to Heywood Allen when he was seventeen. Ben Franklin's pen names were eloquent—it wouldn't have been hard to guess at the tone of a letter from Alice Addertongue or Busy Body.

Sometimes, though, I wonder if the use of a pen name doesn't just arise from fear. My guess is that this is true more often than one might think and more often than most writers who use pen names might care to admit. Fear of failure. Fear of not being accepted. Fear of not belonging to the right social class, the right ethnic group, the right gender—there's some basis in fact to *that* fear, for sure. Aspiring writers often believe that having one's work published is "all a matter of who you know," as if there were a secret society in the publishing world to which they were being denied entry. I can understand the attractiveness of that belief; it protects a writer's ego from the possibility that his or her work needs to be a lot better than it is at present, if it is ever to see the light of day. It is certainly true that the more contacts one has, the better, and that we should use every contact we have. And it is also true that some writers have a head start in being related or otherwise connected to somebody famous. But there are not many of those. Most successful writers were once unconnected unknowns. It wasn't their connections that got them where they are. It was hard work and the gift of words. It was the combination of the two. It was the call.

There are times when time itself stands still. Sometimes it is when a deadline is inches away. In that

fierce contest with the clock, a plea goes up: *Stop the sun,
as you did for Elisha:*

> The sun stopped midheaven, and did not hurry
> to set for about a whole day. There has been
> no day like it before or since, when the Lord
> heeded a human voice.
>
> Joshua 10:13b–14

And it actually happens: prayer breathes through my
desperation, giving me words and sentences and a way to
end—often I don't realize I've written the last sentence
until I read it over and realize that it's enough. *You're finished. Right there. That's the end, right there.* That happens to
me much more often than it does not.

At other times, it's when there's all the time in the
world. You write almost dreamily, spinning out words and
taking them back. Hours pass, and you'd be hard-pressed to
account for the time. One idea shyly suggests another, and
you arrange and rearrange them. You remember your yellow
pads, with all their scratch-throughs, your typewriter, your
clunky dedicated word processor, your first real computer,
your first iPad. The physical tools have changed, but the
skein of words is continuous, miles long, through all these
writing years.

## 2
# ARTIST

**"WHAT ARE YOU DOING TODAY?"** I ask N early this morning. N is a painter. He is an abstractionist—he used to be a realist, painting the kinds of portraits in which you could just about see the individual pores in a subject's skin. He left that behind when he got sober. Too scary.

"Working on paintings nobody wants."

There's some truth to that. Though in recent years he has had some gratifying critical success, N doesn't sell many paintings. When he does, they sell for a lot—tens of thousands—but that only happens once or twice a year. The rest of the time he paints people's apartments. So it's not precisely the case that *nobody* wants them, but I guess it's true that most people don't.

"I say f—k them."

"I'm sure you do."

I love his paintings. I would buy one if I had the money—I do own two, from a time before they commanded the prices they do today. I predict that they will be very valuable after he dies. Somebody is going to make some serious money off of poor old N.

His paintings are too beautiful to be piled up on the sidewalk and end up in the landfill. Beautiful and mysterious. There is little point in asking an abstractionist to talk to you about his paintings. They are not about anything, he says, other than actual painting and drawing. There is no message or narrative. There are no forms. There are barely any shapes—an edge here, a curve there, but none of them lead to any conclusion. We went to Italy together a couple of times; N stayed with us for a few weeks and then returned home to New York to paint. I went over to his place to take a look a few months later. Did he paint the towers of Siena as seen from our house? The vineyards? The Duomo in Florence? No. But a certain curve began to appear in some of his paintings: it was the curve of the lamp brackets on the exteriors of Italian buildings. The lamp brackets—that was it. Being in a beautiful place doesn't make an abstractionist paint the beautiful place. It just makes him paint.

"What should I do with all these paintings when I croak? Put them out on the curb, I guess."

"Well, you won't be doing anything with them. You'll be dead. We'll figure something out." I guess we'd better pay some attention to this question now, though. If N intends to die young, he'd better hurry up.

There are some very successful artists—successful in terms of making lots of money. But they are few in number. There are a few very successful writers, and a few successful actors. There are people in every artistic community who do very, very well. But there are not many in any of them. We may envy other artists' commercial success, but it is unlikely that any of us will achieve it. This is why we don't quit our day jobs.

Admitting up front that a career in the arts will not be

a quick trip to fame and fortune brings us a little nearer to what it means to be called to it. Your art is not a means to an end—it is an end in itself. Your art is not something you hope to become, although your entire life will be spent building and improving the craft of it. Your art is not something you *will* be. It is something you already *are*.

Disappointment is built into the arts. All artists learn to live with rejection, and lots of it. This is not true only in the performing arts, in the cold sweat and nausea of fear as you wait to audition. It's true for all the arts. Artists are tough. Even solitary pursuits like writing or painting are *communicative*. Works of art demand to be shared, and the final step of creating them is acceding to this demand, however much fear and trembling sharing them brings. They won't let you shove them into a drawer and forget about them. They want to be seen. You may dread letting anybody else see them at first, but your need to share your art will win out.

Perhaps this is part of what it means to be called: That to which you are called is stronger than your fear. In the end, you give up the fear. *Ready or not,* you say, *here I come.* What's the worst that can happen? The worst that can happen is that I don't get the part, my painting doesn't sell, the publisher doesn't want my book. But wait—all those things are already true. I already *don't* have the part, I *haven't* sold the painting, I *haven't* sold my book! If my effort does not succeed, my state will be unchanged. So I have nothing to lose.

And it will be over soon enough.

# 3
# TEACHER

**SOMEWHERE IN THIS HOUSE IS A** medal Q got from Rutgers. Probably it's hanging in the living-room closet, with his rusty academic gown. The medal is huge, the size of a dessert plate. I forget now which of Q's teaching anniversaries it marked—thirty years, I think. Maybe thirty-five. Or maybe it was upon his retirement.

All told, Q has taught for more than sixty years. He was taken to his father's offices once or twice when he was young, but it was clear he had no interest in the textile business. His father saw this, and never pressured him to succeed him at the helm. This was a kindness that had not been extended to him by *his* father. Although he was successful at it and led it profitably through the Depression, textiles were never Q's dad's passion—he had trained to be an engineer. His son would be what *he* wanted to be.

"I'm not sure now," he says when I ask Q when it was that he first realized he wanted to teach. "Probably the main reason I went to teach in Turkey after college was because I wanted to see more of the world. I taught English as a second—or fourth, or fifth!—language, at Robert College in Istanbul. It's now called the University of the Bosphorus, but in those days it was an American college. Certainly during the time I was teaching in Turkey, I realized that I loved being part of a faculty. And if I wanted to teach at the university level I would need a doctorate. Then the Korean War started, and I was drafted from Turkey. I applied to graduate school from Germany, where I served, and when I finished my tour of duty I began my work at Yale."

Nearly fifty years later, retirement at the age of seventy was misery for Q. He is an avid gardener, but that didn't come close to filling his days. Going from day to day without a class for which to prepare puzzled him painfully—it was not clear to him why he was here. He lasted four restless years at it, and then returned to the classroom, this time in the continuing education program for seniors that Rutgers has offered for years. The differences between this and teaching undergraduates are all good ones: there are no grades, and the students all want to be there. Nobody sits in the back of the classroom, trying not to be seen by the professor. Students bring the experience of a long lifetime with them into class, and they are eager to contribute. Professors teach what they want to teach. Some of them are retired Rutgers faculty. These days, they receive a small stipend. In the early years of the program, they taught for nothing but the love of it.

"When I was very little, I tried to teach my middle brother to read," says Dorothy, who teaches kindergarten. "I must have been persistent, because when my youngest brother entered kindergarten, my mother suggested I teach him as well. In high school and college I was very involved in drama and choirs—in fact, I started out as a theater major in college, with a minor in education. I switched in the middle of my college career to focus solely on education. I will be forever grateful things turned out as they did. I can't imagine doing a job I could love more.

"I get tired, now that I'm getting older, but I come home with such a sense of satisfaction and accomplishment. In the morning I sit up on the edge of my bed and think, 'Ugh, I've got to go to work.' Then seconds later I start to think about the day and begin to figure out how I'm going to do this or that and I'm already there, before I have even stood up from my bed."

What does she love most about teaching?

"The children—I don't even have to think about that one. I enjoy their company and the way they think and what they have to say. They are such interesting little people. That goes not only for kindergartners but the other grades as well. They all have very complex and interesting ways of thinking. I also love the feeling of confidence I have. I really know what I'm doing and I know I'm good at it."

Elizabeth worked as a substitute teacher for several years after graduating, unable to find a permanent teaching job. When one came up in special education, she recoiled— anything but that! But she took it; maybe something more in line with her desires would come up, she thought. Maybe somebody would go out on maternity leave. *I can do this for a year,* she told herself. You can do anything for a year.

But almost immediately, she fell in love with her students. She was patient. She was good at seeing them as individuals, each a person unlike any other person in the whole world, disabled or not. She was good at rejoicing in their seemingly small victories, recognizing them as the daily triumphs they were. Another position did come up, but she didn't take it. She never wants to do anything else but this, she says now.

Denise more or less fell into her work with children with disabilities. She was substituting at her daughter's school when a permanent paraprofessional position opened there to serve students with autism. Close to home, a convenient fit with her daughter's schedule—these practicalities were the factors that sealed the deal for Denise, not any particular sense of destiny or calling to serve children with disabilities. But like Elizabeth, she fell in love quickly, and forever.

> Looking back, I would say that I really was led to where I am now. I started out with being a paraprofessional for one student, who at the time was in first grade. The following year I was in the same first grade class, because there were a few special education students. A year after that, the principal put me in a self-contained half-day preschool disabled program. A couple of years later Edison opened full-day preschool autistic programs, and I was moved to that class. Over time things have evolved, and now it is called the "full-day preschool disabled class."
>
> Now, as I finish up my sixteenth year in the district, I have been blessed to work with some of the most amazing teachers and fellow paras,

people who come into work every day with the goal of doing the best for their students. I have also been blessed to be able to work with a wonderful group of students, who every day, without fail, put a smile on my face and make me feel so proud of them with everything they do. Yes, there are days when I feel frustrated and ineffective, but without fail, the students shine through.

Maybe we are not always called at the beginning, not in such a way as to know it at the time. But "led," one thing leading to another—a path created by walking.

A path created by walking.

People think of God's plan in terms of causality, but there is more than causality at work in human events. Does God need to cause things in our lives in order for them to be part of our holy journey? There is danger if we answer yes—pursue it far enough and you can end up believing that the bombing of the World Trade Center was part of God's plan because it brought people together, or that someone's AIDS diagnosis was part of God's plan because it led her daughter to become a doctor specializing in infectious disease. Though these may be friendlier beliefs than the ones about God causing terrible things to punish or test us, they are no more reasonable. We need not look for God only at the beginnings of things. The energy that created and creates us is present throughout. It is never absent.

# 4
# DOCTOR

**ORDINARILY A SOBER AND WELL-BEHAVED CHILD,** today two-year-old Henry trotted down the driveway toward the road, naked as a jaybird. His nurse ran after him as fast as she could. "Doc! You git back here right now! Doc!" Already Henry had a nickname that foretold his future: she called him "Doc."

Henry's father had wanted to be a physician. His great-grandfather had been one: the horse-and-buggy kind, traveling the rich Black Belt farmland of northwestern Alabama. This would have been just after what Henry sometimes still calls the War Between the States. In those days, there were many who could not pay. Even those who had been wealthy were not now, and those who had been poor were poorer still. That seems to have been something he decided not to worry about—he just treated everyone who needed him and trusted in God to make it right in the end. God upheld his end: I don't think Henry's grandfather died rich, but he didn't die poor.

Henry's father became a medical corpsman during the First World War, tending the fallen on the front lines in France: applying tourniquets, bandaging wounds, deciding which of the wounded had a chance of surviving and getting those fortunate ones on stretchers and back to the field hospital as fast as he could, leaving the others to die in misery amid the hell that rained down on every man and every animal there. No sooner had he saved one than another fell, and another. Nobody who studies medicine imagines it this way.

When Henry's father came home from France, he had what today we would call PTSD—post-traumatic stress disorder. If you ask me, that's a pretty sterile term for something so hideous: fear and pain have entered your mind and your body and camped there, waking you screaming from fitful sleep, robbing your days of everything but their own poison, souring the creamy sweet milk of all your loves. Some people never get better. Nobody recovers completely.

His was severe enough to land him in Walter Reed Hospital for a few months after the war was over. It took a while for him to heal. But he was young, with his life ahead of him: as devastating as his experience in the war was, it couldn't stop him from wanting to go to medical school, as he had always dreamed of doing.

But his family's strapped finances could. A sharp worldwide recession followed the war. His father had died, and he was the eldest in his family. There was no money to underwrite medical school. He would never become a doctor. He became a pharmacist instead, and kept the family drugstore afloat during that brief economic depression and the Great Depression of the 1930s.

*I cannot imagine the grief he experienced during those times,* his son Henry writes now. But I think he can imagine it, and I think he often does.

At the age of forty-eight, Henry's father died of grievous injuries sustained in a car crash. He lingered for a few days, and twelve-year-old Henry remained by his bedside as much as his relatives would allow. Seventy years later, he remembers everything: how the room looked, how it smelled, how maimed his father was, how he mustered the strength to smile at his son, knowing the little boy's agony was as great as his own. Father and son had been extraordinarily close; Henry was his parents' only child. Henry sat in a chair by the bed and watched in silent misery. After a day or so, he began to pull strands of hair from his own head.

It was not his injuries themselves that killed Henry's father. It was an infection that developed afterwards. Henry noticed that the floor in the hospital room was not clean— "filthy," he calls it as he tells the story. "Filthy." Henry is a self-contained man, more given to understatement than to hyperbole, but his rage quivers in the very word. This terrible loss was preventable. His father need not have died. Had routine sterile procedures been followed faithfully, his father would not have been torn from him.

Asked now if his vocation as a physician might have been, at least in part, a means of replaying his tragedy and giving it a better ending, Henry is noncommittal—he is a cardiologist, not a psychiatrist. But he does admit to the possibility that medicine was a way to carry on his father's unfulfilled dream. "I saw him once," Henry tells me, "at the door of the chapel" on the day that he graduated from the University of the South. Henry had been accepted into the medical school at Tulane and was ready to begin this next chapter of his life. The man stood silhouetted in the doorway, watching Henry receive his diploma. He had his father's stance, his shoulders, he had the same upward tilt of his chin. It was he. When Henry looked again, the man was gone.

Certainly there were less mystical reasons to go into medicine—Henry liked his science classes and made top grades in all of them. He was encouraged by his advisers. He admired upperclassmen in premed studies at Sewanee. They were serious, as he was, ambitious high achievers. "I was a nerd," he remembers, "never smoked or drank all through school, until our graduation banquet at medical school, when I had my very first alcoholic drink of any kind and took a stethoscope to our meanest professor to see if he had a heart."

What might Henry have become, if not a physician? He loved poetry and has read and written it all his life. "If I had not chosen medicine I might have aspired to major in English, pursue creative writing, and probably teach. But I have never regretted my decision. Medicine brought out a side of me that never would have surfaced. As an only child, I was self-centered—medicine taught me to think about others and use my skills to help them. It taught me how to think scientifically and apply knowledge to the benefit of my patients. Developing genuine concern for a patient brought me inward satisfaction I could not have found elsewhere."

The medical profession changed a great deal in the fifty years that Henry was active in it. "The twentieth century was the golden age of medicine, and I am thankful to have been part of it," he tells me. But not every change was for the better.

> I have hated the bureaucracy that has evolved to disrupt the doctor-patient relationship. Already private practice is being eliminated across the country as hospitals buy up groups of doctors. The intervention of the government in many ways had initially some merit, like Medicare, but subsequent policies have undermined the profession. My hope—fading—is that new governmental policies will strive to bring back the doctor-patient relationship, stress the importance of medical ethics and teach the history of the profession. Scholarships to worthy students and a renewed guidance by practicing physicians as mentors could revive the spirit and pride of the profession. If it's not too late.

It's never too late to answer a call, Henry. And he proved it to himself this past summer by earning a Master of Fine Arts in creative writing. He wrote poetry throughout his medical career, publishing seven volumes of it over the years. He tells me that he is the oldest person ever to have received a graduate degree from Sewanee. Henry will be eighty-four next June.

Henry followed the traditional trajectory of a medical career—he started young. Clare had a very different path: She became a physician's assistant after thirty years as an Episcopal priest. This is unusual; we do have a few doctors who have become clergy, but I don't know of many people who have done it in reverse. The first stirrings of a medical vocation came in the midst of her busy years as a parish rector, although I imagine there must have been signs of it earlier than that—Clare's father was a doctor, and medicine runs in families. At first, it seemed impossible: medical school? In middle age? With kids still in school? She may have daydreamed over course catalogues, but that was as far as she thought she could ever go. This would be one of those daydreams about things that might have been.

At the age of forty-two, Clare's husband was diagnosed with cancer. Clare was his primary caregiver. She became intimate with Gerry's body in a new way. "I was taught how to manage the IVs. No needles—he had a port. Just hanging the bag, hooking up the tubes, making sure there wasn't any air in the lines and then disconnecting everything when the bag was empty."

One day, as she changed his IV bag, she received as clear a calling as she had ever had. As clear as the long-ago moment when she first felt the call to ordained ministry. "As clearly as if a voice from heaven had spoken, I knew that this was what I was called to do. And just as clearly I was told that I needed to be a physician assistant, which was a little funny since I didn't know very much about what PAs were or what they did."

Clare called her mom. Then she called a nearby school offering a physician assistant program to ask if there were any other middle-aged students. There were. This wasn't a crazy idea. The training of a physician is long and grueling, and hardly anybody who isn't young begins it. Training to be a PA is grueling, too, but it wouldn't take as long. She could be serving in four years.

Clare had almost twenty more years of ministry left if she wanted them, and many possibilities for those years. She was the right age to become a bishop and had the creativity to be the dean of a cathedral; she had entertained a number of invitations to consider both of those. She was trying to stay open to possibilities, but her heart and her curiosity were not in new positions in the church she'd served for thirty years. She could feel it taking its place in her past.

Though her husband didn't live to see her begin her formal training, he was part of the decision. When she took an early retirement from the ministry, some people probably assumed it was because of her grief at losing him. But this had been in the offing for some time. "Gerry knew I'd been hankering for med school for fifteen to twenty years, and we had also been talking on and off for years about my taking the thirty-year retirement option. We both knew that the odds were not in our favor, that by the time I was actually ready to retire and make the transition, I'd be doing it all alone." Clare's early years of mourning were also years of hard work at something very new, which must have helped her travel through her grief.

I wondered how her two callings compared.

"I have loved discovering that I could actually do science." Clare was trained as an opera singer and is also a playwright. I have never known her to have anything to do with anything remotely scientific. "I love now being able to care for the body as well as the soul. I love understanding how they go together—at the cellular level. I love actually knowing how DNA works, how to read an EKG, suture a laceration, or interpret a blood test. I have loved learning something entirely new."

She hasn't loved becoming a novice again. I can well imagine that—Clare was senior in her profession and widely respected in the church. "It's been very hard to go back to feeling incompetent. After thirty years of parish ministry, I was really good at it, and it's been difficult to feel ignorant and clueless. I actually haven't minded being at the bottom of the food chain, though—if there's one thing I understand, it's hierarchy."

Yup. The church teaches you all about that.

"But I do miss feeling competent."

She misses the Dance of the Priest. But there's a dance in medicine, too. There's a dance in every calling. And she will still be a priest—you never stop being one, no matter what you do for a living. "Indelible" is the word we use for that aspect of our calling. Indelible—like indelible ink. Our vocation can't be erased. How that will play out is not yet clear. Clare expects to be working lots of weekends.

Demetrio began his training later, after a stint in the military, a dozen years in the financial industry, and work as a lay minister in the church.

> At this point in my life, I have tried many professions. I have done reasonably well in all of them. I have enjoyed parts of all of them. All of them have had parts that I did not enjoy. I always got external validation, but I believe that is because I try to put my heart into everything that I do.
>
> I started on the path to my current profession because I thought—I just had an inkling—that maybe medicine would bring together all the things that nourished me from all my previous professions into one. And the more I progressed on this path, the more I knew my thought was right. I felt the call internally—as in, I can't imagine doing with my life anything other than what I am doing with it now. I feel validated in my call because I enjoy every minute of the work that I do, and even though my body is physically exhausted (and many times my mind as well) at the end of a long day of work, my spirit feels nourished. I never felt anything close to this feeling after a long day of work in any

previous profession. People inside and outside of my profession say they can't picture me doing anything else.

I get to heal the broken. That is the greatest gift in the world. I get to bring the gifts I developed in other professions to be a better healer in this one. My previous work in ministry helps me to better connect to people in their time of vulnerability, to really hear what it is that they need from me. My previous career in finance helps me to better understand how the institution of providing health care works, so that I can work behind the scenes as well, to help fix the system to help get more people the care that they need affordably. My previous experience in the military helps me to better navigate the bureaucracy and hierarchy that unfortunately still pervades my new profession. Every experience I have had helps to make me a better healer.

What does Demetrio hate about his new calling? The same thing that frustrates all high achievers: not being able to do it all. "That I can only do so much for so many. There are so many more that I wish I could help. I hope that people continue to trust us to take care of them and that we continue to do good work and to daily earn that trust."

## TO FALL AND RISE AGAIN

On morning rounds
a favorite patient collapses before you
and as you struggle to catch him,
your knees buckle
and you kneel beside him on the floor.
You hold him as part of him dies
as others who are dying there
but you walk away stronger
for having touched him.
Perhaps it is all they need from you:
to fall a bit
when they begin to fall
and to rise again with them.
Sometimes, it is what you need
to rise again
from your own despair,
to remember who you once were,
who you are.

                              Henry Langhorne, M.D., 2015

5

# WAITER

**MY DAUGHTER SCARED THE LIVING DAYLIGHTS**
out of me a few years after she finished college: She quit a
well-paying job with medical benefits to become a waitress.
She had been a publicist in the music business, which was an
exciting job for a young woman, at first—rock stars, parties, concerts. It began to pall after a time, though. How
excited can a person continue to be about yet another nine-
teen-year-old's debut CD? And what about that might make
the world a better place? She knew she was dispirited where
she was but didn't yet know what might bring her spirit
back to life. There was only one way to find out.

"I'm going to work at O'Flaherty's," she said over
dinner one night. I knew the place. It was a few blocks from
her apartment.

"That's a nice place," I said, evenly. It wasn't Lutèce, but
it was decent. I used to take young actors there sometimes.
Most of the waitstaff were actors.

"For now, I need a job that won't demand lots of con-
centration and that constant availability. Something I can just
do and then come home. I need to think about what I want
for my life."

"Okay." This was before young adults could stay on their
parents' medical insurance policies until age twenty-six. I

was trying not to focus on that. What else could I say? Anna was a grown woman.

It turned out that she liked O'Flaherty's. "I really liked being a waitress," she says now, looking back. "I remember how much I loved all the church suppers when I was little. That was always my favorite part of church. I really liked waiting on people. O'Flaherty's was kind of like that."

Anna's fighting weight was 125 pounds. She went down to 115 while she worked at O'Flaherty's: Waiting tables is hard physical work. She was there for a couple of years while she thought about her future. Then she applied to graduate school in education. Today she is a teacher.

"Do you remember anything anybody said when you told them you were leaving to go back to school?"

"Not specifically. They were all happy for me. I could sense some sadness in a few people though, people who felt stuck there or didn't know what was next for them. Bars are filled with missed opportunities."

"They are," I said. "But was there anyone there who seemed to you to have a real vocation for the work? For whom it was absolutely where they were meant to be?"

Anna answered right away.

"The two older bartenders. But you know, I'm not sure. They were both Irish from Ireland—they may have just not had many choices in the US. But both of them were so smart, and they were amazing storytellers. They could've done anything. It was nice knowing some old guys were behind the bar. Old, but not afraid to pick up a bat if need be."

A ladies' lunch: one great-granddaughter, one grand-daughter, my daughter, and me. Just girls. In deference to the youngest member of our party, we go to a place where they are sure to serve chicken fingers. We slide into a booth.

Our waitress comes to take our order. She is not much younger than I am. I was a waitress when I was young, and it was hard work even then: the hours on your feet, the heavy trays of full plates. My initial reaction to seeing a woman in her late middle age doing this work is to wish she didn't have such a physically demanding job.

But then I remember a woman I met when I was in seminary. I was a student chaplain then, and she was about the age I am now. That day I was assigned to the ICU. She sat up in her hospital bed, the head of it raised as far as it would go. She was going to a regular hospital room in just a little while, she told me with a smile, and then she was sure to be going home soon.

"I can't wait to get back to work!"

"Really? What do you do for a living?"

"I'm a waitress. I really miss my restaurant." She had been a waitress for forty years, since before the war, and had been at this restaurant for twenty-five of them.

"Bet you're a great waitress."

"I am a good waitress, if I do say so. The same ones come in the restaurant every day—I know what they want before they even say hello."

"You miss them?"

"I do. And they miss me. Those are my boys."

We talked on. She had never married, and her parents had died long ago. She had a married sister in another state, but it was obvious that the people in the restaurant were her real family now and had been for years. She grew a little less upbeat as the conversation continued—the doctor had told her that she might not be able to go back right away. Truth to tell, it seemed likely to me that she might *never* go back to such heavy work, since she was in the hospital for a heart attack, but I didn't say so. I could see her natural optimism struggle with the very real threat of a new loneliness in her near future, perhaps for the rest of her life.

She told me about coming here from Ireland as a girl, and about living in Hell's Kitchen. Her father worked on the waterfront. Her mother was a laundress. She used to go to people's homes to do their washing and hang it out to dry.

"Back then, we hung our laundry out the window on a clothesline that went across the alley, you know," she said. "It was on a pulley. All up and down the street you would see the shirts and overalls and diapers overhead, flapping in the breeze. They don't let you do that now, you know. I remember walking down the street from school and seeing my mother in a different neighbor's window every day, hanging out wash. My sister could whistle really loud, and she would whistle so my mother would look down and see us and wave."

She laughed at the memory. She spun stories from her girlhood every time I saw her, which was more times than either of us hoped it would be that first day. She didn't go home as soon as she thought she would, and she didn't get her doctor's permission to go back to work. I wonder if she ever did. I hope, if she couldn't, that she became a hostess there. Or even one of the regular customers. Why not? They were family.

That's what being a waiter is, at its best. It is a way of showing hospitality, of honoring one who has come under a roof that is, in some sense, yours. *Welcome to McDonald's,* says a disembodied voice at the drive-through window. The voice may belong to a worker at a call center in Calcutta, but the phrase references a contractual relationship: *I am your host and you are my guest. This isn't just a sale and purchase. It is the ancient welcome of the innkeeper to the traveler: For your time here, your well-being is my charge.*

"I'll tell you about a waiter," Kathy told us at lunch while we talked about this. "When I first came to New York, I lived with a friend who was a nurse. I slept on her rug—oh boy, my back hurts just thinking of it now! We were young and none of us had any money, so we always got a slice of pizza and a beer at the pizzeria down the block from her apartment, which was near the hospital.

"But the waiter there was unbelievable—he was like a waiter at the restaurant in the world. He would place our pizza slices before us as if they were the most expensive meal in town. He would pour our beer into a glass with such smoothness, such elegance! Here we were, these young women without a dime, but he treated us like queens. I can see him now, brushing the crumbs away from the Formica table like we were in an exclusive restaurant. And it was just a local pizza joint."

I am sitting at Hailey's with an iced tea, waiting for my lunch to arrive. It is Saturday afternoon, and I had a wedding this morning. There was a time when I wouldn't have been worn out from one wedding, but that was a while back. After this I intend to go home and take a nap.

I am not at my usual table in the corner—I want to be able to see the musician. Most nights and weekend days there is live music at Hailey's, music of all kinds—jazz on Sunday afternoons, Irish music on a couple of weeknights, louder stuff on Friday and Saturday nights. This afternoon it's a young man with a guitar, singing songs from my daughters' youth, not my own. His program reminds me of being in the car with the girls, of our contests of wills about whose favorite radio station would accompany our drive to school.

The walls and ceiling of Hailey's are festooned with the county flags of Ireland, each bearing the heraldic symbol of the county and its name, in English and in Irish. Posters advertising Guinness and other brands, framed photographs of the Irish coast and the Irish countryside alternate with blackboards upon which today's specials from the kitchen are listed, along with craft beers and specialty cocktails, in a quantity and variety somewhat greater than one might expect in a neighborhood pub. An electronic sign over one of the chalkboards counts down the days, hours, minutes, seconds, and tenths of seconds until next St. Patrick's Day—the count will begin anew at 12:01 a.m. on March 18.

Compared to what it will be like tonight, when they close off Main Street and Hailey's moves outside to become an outdoor beer garden, it's quiet in here: a couple of regulars at the bar, a family with two young boys at a table in back and a few other diners. One waiter easily handles us all— everyone else is busy setting up tables and kegs for the beer garden.

A pub in a small town is a little like a church: an egalitarian place in which all are welcome and everyone is glad to see everyone else. One can be as quiet or as social as one pleases here. People chat at the bar or sit with a friend at the small tables; some sit and watch games on the several television screens fastened high up on the wall. The occasional shout goes up to announce a score. I come alone; I like to sit in the corner and write. I have always enjoyed writing in a corner of the room while human activity is going on around me, as long as it's not human activity in which I must maintain a speaking part.

The proprietor manages the mood of the place with an invisible hand, with the result that I have never seen an obviously intoxicated person at Hailey's. I sit down with Chris on his day off, so that he can have a beer while we talk. I never thought about that, but of course he doesn't drink when he's on duty.

What I want to talk to him about is the vocation of hospitality. It seems to me that Chris has it: he was born to run a neighborhood establishment like this, a place where people come to relax and enjoy one another. He is like that great waitress I met all those years ago: happiest when he is welcoming.

"What did you do before you opened Hailey's?"

"I was twenty years on Wall Street. I did well, but I wasn't passionate about it like I am about this place." I'd like to say that here Chris took a long reflective drink of beer, but the truth was he never got to have a beer today, at least not while I was there. It's supposed to be his day off, but he's had two meetings with contractors already today and it's only noon. In about a month, Hailey's is going to open a gaming arcade in a storefront around the corner, so there's a lot to do. That's another way in which Chris's vocation is a lot like mine was. I often didn't get to take my day off, either. And there's another way: I worked on Christmas Day, too. Hailey's opens up in the afternoon on Christmas and Thanksgiving. Not the kitchen, just the bar; the kitchen crew is off to be with their families on the holiday. On Christmas Day, Chris tends the bar by himself.

"I'm no bartender. If someone wants a special martini, he's out of luck." But he can pull a beer well enough.

"You know how after Thanksgiving dinner people will say, I'm going out for a walk? Well, some of them end up here. And then there are people in town who don't have families to go to. Some of them bring food and we'll heat it up for them."

I sit at my corner table until the place begins to fill up in the late afternoon. Soon it will be time for me to go home and start cooking supper. Chris moves through the place, reminding me of myself at coffee hour back in the parish. I used to love watching people talk and laugh, noting who seemed to be sitting alone and then doing something about it, catching up with people. It seemed to me to be a bit like the kingdom of God, which is so often compared in the Bible to a banquet. But a banquet is pretty formal. Maybe the kingdom of God is more like a neighborhood pub.

I remembered Anna telling me about the two older bartenders who kept a bat behind the bar. I asked Chris if he had a bat.

"No comment," he says with a laugh. But then he continues, "See that stick up there on the wall behind the bar? That's a shillelagh."

"You know how to use it?"

"Yeah. But I've never had to. I never let it get that far."

Chris views drinking as a privilege, not a right. "Just because you can afford to drink doesn't mean you're good at it. If you can't treat people with respect and talk without making every other word the F-bomb, we're just not your place. There are plenty of other bars you can go to."

Hailey's is safe. Single women can come here and know they won't be hassled. Parents can bring the Little League team here and know they won't see something they shouldn't. In its seven years of existence, Hailey's has never had to call the police.

In the winter, the preteen students of an Irish dancing school sometimes perform on a Sunday afternoon. That's usually a quiet time at the pub, but once the parents and grandparents of the little dancers have taken their seats, the place is packed. Witnessing this once, I feared for everyone's safety when the music began—how on earth were the girls going to be able to dance in this crowd? But I had forgotten what Irish dance is like: Irish dancers keep their arms locked at their sides. They don't take up much room, and they don't travel; just the legs move, and they move with blinding speed.

Afterwards, the families dine together. The little girls are hungry, and happy about their performance. Sunday evening will be a quiet one at the pub; a devoted crowd comes in at four to sit at the bar and play trivia. I sit in my corner and listen, but do not contribute.

**Q.** What was the name of the "woman he loved" for whom Edward VIII abdicated the throne of England?

**A.** Wallis Simpson. I can't believe nobody knew that one. Then again, I'm the oldest person here.

**Q.** What is the common name for the chemical compound sodium chloride?

**A.** Table salt.

**Q.** What was the name of B. B. King's guitar?

**A.** Lucille.

I do not know what the winner receives, if anything. I imagine it's a free drink. But maybe it's just the thrill of victory. I'll have to ask Chris, next time I come. But it's time to go home now, for me.

# 6
# ACTOR

**I FIRST MET DANA ON THE** radio. His was the lovely baritone voice I sometimes encountered instead of the regular hosts of my favorite programs on WQXR. He offered more than the disembodied intellect the FM radio voice usually gives us: There was a person behind the sound. Then our paths crossed at Trinity Wall Street, where Dana directed staged readings for Theatre at Trinity. Our circles of theater friends in New York overlapped often. A lot of people knew Dana. He was one of those actors you meet a lot there: journeyman actors, who cobble together a living out of large and small parts in whatever shows they can get, calling their agents and pounding the pavement in between gigs, always in search of the next show. Like all the arts, the theater is a noble profession but a hard business. The ladder of professional advancement in theater is more like a labyrinth; I know an actor who had a starring role in a TV series that ran for several years and now considers himself lucky to have landed an antacid commercial, for which they painted a diagram of the human digestive tract on his well-toned abdomen. Acting is not for sissies. There are some for whom success is a straighter shot, but a convoluted journey of fits and starts is much more common.

I was often the beneficiary of this harsh reality. The productions I directed or produced were small and low budget. But wonderful actors were glad to have the chance to play a classic role for me, knowing they would probably never play that role on Broadway or in Central Park—the starring roles there go to people who are already stars. A chance to be Hamlet, to be Becket in *Murder in the Cathedral* or the psychiatrist in *Agnes of God*—often almost all I could offer was that one-line addition to their resumes, and a place to satisfy their desire to do what they became actors to do. But they took it gladly and gave it their all, for love of their craft. Again and again, they gave me much more than I had any right to expect.

Dana was one of those. His day job was actually at night—he was a proofreader for a large legal practice; each morning, a crew of them had all the documents produced during the day ready for the next day's business. He procured jobs at the same place for a number of his younger friends—Dana was like that, happy to mentor and offer help to younger actors. This one was perfect—they could come in and out of the cadre of proofreaders, leave when they got a show, and return when it ended. The day job is a slippery slope for actors. Many disappear into theirs—a steady paycheck and medical benefits are powerful lures. Dana never did—his clarity about the priority of acting in his life was permanent. He lived within the very limited means his life's choices dictated, in one of the few single-room-occupancy hotels left in New York. It's gone now, metamorphosed into an expensive boutique hotel. But it was full of actors and other artists in those days. They had other things on their minds besides their decor.

Dana was a wonderful colleague and friend. I do know that it was hard to be closer than that to him—temporary relationships centered on the theater worked best for him. Here is how he explained it:

> I grew up in a threadbare family: no father, a difficult and demanding mother, a brother and sister who were a decade and more older than I. I suffered a great lack of the feelings and experiences of a family life. Hence I tried to make a family out of whatever theater company I was with. I tried thinking of them as my fathers and mothers, my sisters and brothers, and, eventually, my sons and daughters. Of course it didn't work. They all had families somewhere, and other lives. When I retired, it was my destiny to live alone and lonely. But it was also the time to start learning about, understanding, and appreciating myself. The party is going on, the games are being played and the crowd may be fun to be with, but you won't find yourself there. You will find yourself in the vast, bright, mysterious, and sacred cathedral of your own mind.

Dana wanted an imaginary family to become real, but couldn't cope with a real one. His was a solitary life, at the end—this, although he had a son who lived in California about whom I knew next to nothing. Dana had moved out of New York to the Pennsylvania town in which he did his last show in a regional theater. He lived happily there on his pension from Actors Equity and Social Security. Within a few years, his health began to deteriorate. He walked with difficulty, and used a cane.

Some friends facilitated his admission into the Actor's Home in New Jersey, higher up on the waiting list than he would have been. This was no mean feat. They drove him up there. Dana took a look. He wrote me about the visit. Everybody there was in wheelchairs! They had all given up! This was no place for him! He made his friends drive him home, and was angry at them ever after. *He had a way of just walking away from people when (he felt) they asked too much from him,* another mutual friend wrote me. I guess this was one of those times.

*Oh Dana, No!* I thought; *this is your one chance for a safe place with people to take care of you.* I wrote him back, saying that it would take real courage to make such a change, and that I knew he had that kind of courage.

But no.

"What kind of courage does it take to sit in a wheelchair?" he demanded. "These people have all given up. Where's the courage in that?" I guess Dana hadn't known many people with disabilities. If he had, he might have had a more complete understanding of what courage is.

I wrote back that I was talking about the courage it takes to accept a reality we don't want to acknowledge. Wrong answer. He did not reply, and I didn't hear from him for a while. When I did, it was with a surprising message: Dana was going to go back to New York. He was going to work again! Did I know of an accessible place he could afford?

*Afford.* In *New York.* Rents had been ridiculously high when he left town and had gone through the roof since then. *Afford.* And *accessible.* Oh, boy.

I mentioned a place in the theater district where rents were subsidized for artists, but I knew they had a long waiting list. And Dana knew it, too. Everybody in the business knows about it, and they all want to live there. The place where he used to live had become a chichi hotel; rooms there now go for $500 a night. Besides, Dana could barely walk now. Moving back to New York to act was an insane idea. But he was hopeful. Dana was hopeful. It wasn't too long afterwards that I had a message that he was gravely ill and in the hospital, and then that he had died. He never left Pennsylvania. His last Facebook posting bleakly reflected his self-exile: *I'm alone in a strange place. I want to know where my people are. I've lost my tribe.*

Ah, me. People die like they live. Not only does an actor count on what is called the willing suspension of disbelief in his audience, he sometimes also cultivates it in himself. Dana did. I guess sometimes the odds against them are too steep for much reality.

They don't all, though. Bart was an actor and director when I knew him in New York. Really gifted, like hundreds of others there—no, probably thousands. It's where you want to be if you're an actor: all the shows are there, and all the agents, all the classes. But it's also where all the good actors are, so the competition is fierce. You were the star of every show your little theater put on back in Ohio, but everyone you meet here was also the star of every show in Little Rock or Tuscaloosa or Duluth. They see the same people over and over again at their auditions: all the ingenues, all the handsome young tenors, all the comics, all come out for the same parts. Beginning actors and directors in New York are entrepreneurial: they form theater companies and put on plays in any way they can, anywhere they can—church basements, laundromats, bars, empty storefronts. They act in one another's plays. You've heard of Shakespeare in the Park? There is also Shakespeare in the Parking Lot, which has been around for at least fifteen years and has gotten a reputation for some very good work. In an active parking lot. Yes.

Bart was part of that scene for a number of years, and enjoyed the same tincture of excitement and frustration that every young theater professional knows all about. Gathering audience is the hardest part of theater in this city, in which there is so much competition. You do wonderful work, and only a handful of people ever see it. About ten years ago, Bart left New York—*left New York!*—to become artistic director of a performing arts center in a high school in Kentucky. He has no regrets about the move, incomprehensible as it seemed to many of his friends at the time.

"When I was in New York, I was helping create incredible art—that went unnoticed. But here, everything we do, no matter how small, is making seismic changes in the lives of others in our community."

In Hardin County, everyone who cares about the arts sees everything he does.

So was Bart called to a life in the theater? He thinks so. "Although I certainly didn't know it at the time. I was just following my passions. I believe we all serve God in different ways. For that matter I believe we all serve different Gods, but that they are the same God in a different way—if that makes sense."

I'm not sure I got that last part.

"I guess what I'm saying is that we are directed by a moral compass. We all know when we lose our way and choose to continue down the wrong or right path on our own. I certainly still head down the wrong path from time to time, but my moral compass—or God—pulls at me like a magnet to head back down the right path. That 'pull' to me is the 'call.'"

Okay. Now I get it: we answer the same call, to be all that we have been created to be, each of us in different ways. There is something else Bart says that reminds me of my own call, the general nature of it, and the chance to help others be absolutely everything they can be. A thing that I liked about directing, in view of my own limitations as an actor: There is a selflessness about the best directors, as there is about the best priests. They are all about their people and not about themselves. They're not going to be the ones on stage. They are realistic about who they are and who they aren't. Maybe that's just something about the best people, period—priests, directors, bosses, all of us.

"I was fortunately blessed with many talents—I didn't excel at any of them, however. The performing arts gave me the opportunity to use all those talents. I have another ten years in my current occupation and then I hope to be able to afford to semi-retire and work across the country as an actor or director—with any luck perhaps it will be for students I have taught."

That's a happy thought.

Barbara just turned eighty. She gets more work in films and commercials than she did when she was young. Violet died last year. She started out in vaudeville and was still getting work into her nineties. So, Bart, ten years from now, twenty years from now—I can see him already. He is gray at the temples. He travels here and there, directing a show for a former student who now runs a theater, playing a middle-aged man in a play written by another alum. I can see him already.

7

# PSYCHOLOGIST

**GORDON'S FATHER WAS AN ECONOMIST, SO**
Gordon became one. Actually, it was a little more compli-
cated than that: he might have been drawn to psychology
sooner, as an undergraduate, but it seemed to him that "psychology was mostly about rats." Economics seemed appeal-
ingly rational. Gordon got his doctorate and taught for a
time. Also in this period, though, he began psychotherapy
and was immediately excited about the landscape of self-
discovery he encountered. Another doctorate, this one in
clinical psychology, and Gordon had found the calling in
which he would spend the next thirty years.

"I very much loved my work. It met my needs and
interest in understanding things and helping others understand them too. And, since I had no children, I got to be in
a parent role and help people grow, partly by re-parenting
them. And I got a chance to teach by training and super-
vising students and to become a leader in the psychological
association and advocate for mental health issues."

But was he *called* to it? A guiding premise of his profession has been that a person's internal processes drive
her beliefs and actions as much or more than any current
external force, which makes Gordon skeptical of the notion
of being "called" to something.

"I'm not sure about being 'called'—what that means.

My habit as a psychologist is to look for the motivating factors behind a decision or to see the needs that are met. But is that a calling? I think of a calling as coming from outside. I do believe, though, in my soul having an intention for purpose in this life, what I need to learn in order to grow."

It wouldn't be hard to understand Gordon's early choice of economics as a combination of wanting to be closer to his father and trying to please him, but it also touched important parts of him that transcended his relationship with his dad—the "soul" to which he refers. Gordon is a born learner and a natural teacher. "I loved good teachers and wanted to be like them. They also were visible at the front of the room and got everyone's attention, which was also appealing!"

My own profession called briefly to him from outside himself, but found no resonance within him.

"My mom was very interested in religion and wanted me to become an Episcopal priest. I was quite connected to the church when I was young but wasn't drawn to the priesthood." This was a good thing for a young person to know about himself—there are enough people, who believe themselves called to it and aren't, that someone who knows he isn't should be respected in that belief and left alone.

But the part of priesthood that involves understanding, supporting, and encouraging people one-on-one: Gordon would have been good at that. As a psychologist, he got to do that in spades. The mentoring part—he would have shone at that, too, and was able to do lots of it, continuing even after retirement from clinical practice. The long hours wouldn't have bothered him——Gordon had an enormous caseload. Would he have been a good preacher? Only if he could have refrained from making the awful puns for which he is famous among his friends. I doubt if he could have pulled that off—— if he had had a pulpit, he would not have been able to resist. His excellent wife and I shudder to think of it. In his practice, Gordon became very interested in what a theologian would call "spirit" and psychotherapy calls "energy work." He studied deeply in Eastern traditions of meditation and healing, adding insights he gained there to his therapeutic toolbox.

The extraordinary attention a therapist must pay to the experience of a client in many, many sessions is beyond the scope of what a priest in a parish can do. We can be spiritual guides over many years and understanding friends in a crisis. We can accompany joys and sorrows in prayer and liturgy. We can offer words of hope in sermons. But we can't spend hours and hours over months and months with one parishioner——we would be unable to attend to the rest of our many duties. We are not trained in the careful picking apart of the layers that make up the self, although most of us know something about it from our pastoral training and from self-exploration in our own psychotherapy. I didn't prescribe medication for my parishioners when they became ill. I didn't set their broken bones. I wanted the best for my parishioners, and that desire entailed knowing when I didn't have what they needed myself.

Gordon accompanied people on the journeys that would

take them closer to the place in which they were their best selves. Gently, he pulled aside curtain after curtain, allowing them the time it took to gather the strength to see what was behind each one. He encouraged people to do and be things they thought they could never do or be. He contemplated the energy of the universe, and allowed himself to be its conduit. He spent happy decades doing it. It used every bit of who he was.

If that isn't a calling, there may be no such thing.

# 8
# LAWYER

**WHEN BARBARA FIRST THOUGHT OF BECOMING**
a lawyer, it was as a career defending the innocent.

"Initially, I thought I was called to fight injustice and to make the world a fairer and better place. I thought that would be accomplished as an attorney, through representing people, primarily in criminal actions. Instead I ended up in civil litigation. But I still had the opportunity to represent people, learn about court and arbitration procedures, and to make sure a fair result was reached."

Now Barbara is an arbitrator—parties to disputes come to her in order to avoid the expense and delay of going to trial. Sometimes her arbitration is binding, if the parties agree in advance to be bound, and sometime it is advisory. "I must be a fair and objective person who determines cases that come before me. I never imagined that I would have to be a broadminded, neutral person, and I certainly never imagined how difficult it could be. . . . I cannot make any determination until every argument and piece of evidence is presented. I must suspend all judgment until the very end of the case."

It must be hard, for someone who was trained to be an advocate. A friend who became a judge joked that he sometimes fought the urge to object during a trial. But after twenty years as an attorney, Barbara knows arbitration to be her call.

The stresses of advocacy were painful at times. Sometimes her own beliefs and the goals of her clients collided, and an attorney's duty in such a case is clear—you represent your client. As time passed, she learned to refuse such a position without fear. It might not have made her friends, nor did it make her any money, but it helped her sleep at night. She was disheartened by the combative and disrespectful way in which some people in the profession treated others. "I have often experienced an 'end justifies the means' mentality in the legal profession. I am always impressed when people do not use that tactic."

That's kind of sad, that it should be noteworthy when someone doesn't act like a narcissistic jerk. There may be something to all those lawyer jokes.

"I think that there needs to be an oath for attorneys, much like doctors to 'do no harm,' particularly to their clients and to the public at large."

Arbitration is better for Barbara. Unlike litigation, it is explicitly anti-pugilistic—it is about finding a solution, not winning a battle. "What I have loved the most is dealing with people and working through legal problems. Each case has a different nuance due to the people and factual situations that are involved. You always walk away with the feeling that you have learned something."

And about those lawyer jokes? There is hope.

"As the public becomes more educated in legal matters, I hope that attorney ethics can be improved. I see a future where people are able to take care of many of their own small legal problems. Attorneys will have to become more knowledgeable in specialized areas of law in order to be successful."

Hmmm. I believe there are currently a million lawyers in the United States. That's a lawyer for every 300 of us, including babies. Maybe there won't be so many in the future. The word "attorney" doesn't come from the medieval practice of settling disputes by means of a jousting tournament, but we view it as if it did. We look at a legal case as if it were a war, as if a clearly defined winner and a clear loser were an indispensable part of coming to terms. But maybe it doesn't have to be that way. The real origin of the word "attorney" is in the Old French word *atorner*, which literally means "turn to" or "assign." Not someone who is willing to cut someone else to ribbons for you and you alone, but someone who is part of a team charged with guiding everyone toward an outcome everyone can accept. It has always interested me that Jesus is sometimes called our "advocate," and we view this as if he were our attorney.

> But if anyone does sin, we have an advocate with the Father, Jesus Christ the righteous, and he is the atoning sacrifice for our sins, and not for ours only but also for the sins of the whole world. . . .
>
> 1 John 2:1b–2

But Jesus is not *assigned* this relationship with us. We didn't retain him. Advocacy is different from litigation—the advocate is immersed in the struggle itself, rather than in a code of rules concerning the struggle. The advocate doesn't go home at the end of the day; he remains in the struggle for as long as it takes. He makes our struggle his own.

9

# CALLED TO JUST PICK UP AND LEAVE

> Now the Lord said to Abram, "Go from your
> country and your kindred and your father's
> house to the land that I will show you."
>
> Genesis 12:1

**THEY'RE GOING TO CANAAN, WHICH IS** where they had been headed years before with Abram's father, Terah. For reasons we do not know, they had stopped and settled in Haran for what sounds like a fair amount of time, long enough to do well there, to prosper and accumulate many more animals and servants. Life was good. But then Terah died, and now it was time to resume the journey.

Abram is head of the family now. After an explicit call from God, he just starts walking, without knowing where he's going. This is so breathtaking an act of faith and courage that, centuries later, St. Paul will remember it this way: *And he believed the Lord; and the Lord reckoned it to him as righteousness* (Rom. 4:3). To go forth in faith was the same thing as having done a good deed. It wasn't just brave—apparently, it was righteous.

But we don't know the whole backstory here. Every story has a backstory, the matrix of whatever is going on that provides the reason for the unfolding action. Life was good in Haran, it seems, but something was going on in Abram's world that needed to change. We just don't know what it was.

We do know that he didn't just sit in his backstory. Whatever needed to change, he experienced an urgent and immediate call to change it now, unmistakable enough that he acted upon it without question. Without fully understanding it. People who knew him may have thought he was crazy. The writer doesn't say.

Change it now.

Wait—

Maybe when I retire.

Maybe when the kids are grown.

Maybe when I pay off the car loan.

Maybe when I get the garage cleaned out.

I can't change it now.

I'll change it later.

No.

The call isn't coming later. Change it now.

The call came to me on an airplane flying home from Switzerland with my musician husband of five years. We were both born and raised Californians and vowed on our marriage day that we would never leave our home, especially not to move to Nashville. As I was sitting in coach next to him, a thought so strong came into my head that without thinking it immediately came blurting out of my mouth. I looked and him and said, "We have to move to Nashville." This declaration stunned me and left him in absolute disbelief.

There was a backstory here, too. There always is. Bobbie's husband was on the road more than he wasn't.

John went on the road and was gone about 260 days out of the year. My business became all-consuming. . . . I stayed home one day to work from home and while I was there, the cleaning woman came to clean; the pool man came to work on the pool. Then the gardener showed up to mow the lawn, the dry cleaners came to deliver and pick up the clothes and, as if that wasn't enough, a pink truck pulled into the driveway to give my two cocker spaniels a wash and a haircut. I looked around and realized that I was working so hard to pay for all of these people to do the things that I could not do, because I was working so hard. I knew a change was needed.

And a country music singer needs to be in Nashville, I guess, if he ever wants to see his family. They bought a house in Nashville which Bobbie'd only seen on a video one of the band members took for her. This was in the early 1990s, so there was no YouTube, no smart phones—the guy mailed her a VHS. Bobbie locked up her California house and drove away.

> I drove across country with a dog, a cat, and my sixteen-year-old son who was going into his junior year of high school, swearing he was going to charge me with child abuse for making him leave his teenage life . . . But I had the sense that we were suspended on this long stretch of road and something far greater than I was guiding every mile. We arrived at our new home to find that John had made it back from his band travels. I fell into his arms completely exhausted. We have lived in this home for the past 25 years and I love it as much as I did the day I saw it. It is the only home that has ever felt this way to me.

Bobbie must be a fantastic realtor—she had built a very successful business back in California and set about doing the same thing in Tennessee. Today she's a leader in her profession.

Bobbie's call was so clear and distinct! So different from my gradual one, but then of course: God is complex enough to call different people to different things in different ways. And calls continue, calls within a call, for all of us. Moving to Nashville wasn't the last big decision Bobbie ever had to make.

> I have found that life presents obstacles and opportunities, usually in that order. I always have a choice of one or several doors that appear to open, when the need is greatest. I have found that one of the opportunities will have such a strong pull and provide me the opportunity to actually envision myself experiencing it. Many times this has been against what I thought I had wanted and actually a more fearful, riskier choice. Yet the pull is so strong, I cannot let it go. I have come to believe that this is the connection that the God of the universe draws upon to unite and lead us all. After experiencing this pull, and succumbing to it, regardless of my fear, I have come to allow myself to trust this force and walk confidently through the door.

Spooky things can happen when a call is sudden, too. Remember Bobbie's house in California?

> It became apparent that I needed to sell our home in California. The market there was beginning to decline and homes were not selling

very quickly and prices were dropping. There were also several floor plans just like ours on the market and they were not selling.

One day she had a strange experience.

I felt a very strong urge to get off the interstate at the exit of my real estate office. As I was driving along, I told myself that I was tired, needed to get to bed, that I would be there in the morning. As the exit approached, the pull got stronger. Just as I almost passed it, I jerked the car across the solid white line and headed off to my office. I was so aggravated, because I thought this was just a stupid compulsive dysfunction on my part. When I got there, standing outside at the entrance were two of my peers. . . . My friend Anthony said, "I have just finished showing my clients from out of town all of the Plan 85 floor plans that are on the market and they do not like any of them." I said, "Funny you mention this; I am planning on putting mine for sale tomorrow!" He said, "Don't do it—let me show it to them first." They loved it, and immediately made me a very generous offer and it closed in 30 days. Not long after that, the earthquake hit and this home was demolished. I found out from friends that these people had taken out earthquake insurance and were well protected. I had not taken out that insurance and would have lost everything, including a successful real estate business, as nothing sold for many months and it took years for this area to return to normal.

I felt as if I had just walked away as a survivor from a plane crash.


Good Lord.

Maybe the difference between sudden, explicit calls, like Bobbie's, like Abram's, like Moses'—and more gradual ones like mine isn't in how God initiates them. Maybe it's in how we receive them. And whether or not we respond.

## 10

# THE CALL

**ABOUT HALF OF THE PEOPLE WHO** come to see me are discerning a professional direction in their lives. They are aware that something needs to change, but are not sure what it is. Or they are sure, but the prospect of making such a change seems impossible. Many are discerning a vocation to priesthood or diaconate. A few have come discerning a call to the vowed religious life in a convent or monastery.

They want help in recognizing a call. As you have noticed throughout this book, different people have different ideas about what a call is, or even if it exists. Does it arise from outside us? Is it God speaking to us? Some of the people I've written about here have heard their calling in just that way. Others have experienced it more internally. Some saw it take shape as history unfolded, one thing leading to another in a trajectory more visible after the fact than before.

Many times, people who are discerning a decision about a path have shared with me a concern that there will be punishment in the offing if they fail to respond to a call from God. After all, when God asks you to do something, shouldn't you do it? Well, yes—but not because you think you'll get a spanking if you don't. Or that all your projects other than the one connected to your call will assuredly fail. I have suggested in this book and elsewhere that our flawed locating of God in the linear time we experience as our reality impairs our understanding of how it is we are rooted in God's love.

We think God's love is like our love—that blend of sentiment, preference, and need we think of when we say the word "love." We realize, eventually, that this is inadequate; it fails to do justice to the omnipotence of the Creator of the universe. So we try to do better, and add the element of self-giving—comparing the love of God to the most sacrificial love we know, that of a parent for a child. Yet even this fails to capture what the love of God really is, and the notion of call suffers as a result. So we try again: the Incarnation, we say, brings God into the very sinews of a human being. That most of the early heresies in the church's history rested upon trying to make sense of just how it was that God became human tells us that we need to continue our search for language about the love of God.

We are helped in our discernment of call if we remember God's words to Moses from the burning bush. "Say this to the people of Israel, 'I AM has sent me to you'" (Exod. 3:17). God doesn't have a name. God is existence itself, the very energy of the universe. Everything that is, exists in God. All times and all places that have ever been and ever will be, exist in God. There is nothing outside of God. This includes you and all your thoughts and desires and certainly your doubts as well—if they exist at all, they exist in God.

We are not capable of perceiving this fact in our current way of being. Instead, we imagine a God who resembles us in many ways but is stronger, smarter, and lives far away from here. But the fact is that God is here now or, as Jesus put it, "The kingdom of God is within you" (Luke 17:21). There is no place that God does not inhabit.

Take heart, then, in your exploration of your calling. It is not a test which you must pass. Do not dread getting the wrong answer. Do not fear disappointing God. Discerning your call is not a trick question. It grows from the very fact of who you are. The very fact of your puzzling over it is part of it. It is—by definition—holy.

## THE CALL

Come, my Way, my Truth, my Life:
Such a Way, as gives us breath:
Such a Truth, as ends all strife:
Such a Life, as killeth death.

Come, my Light, my Feast, my Strength:
Such a Light, as shows a feast:
Such a Feast, as mends in length:
Such a Strength, as makes his guest.

Come, my Joy, my Love, my Heart:
Such a Joy, as none can move:
Such a Love, as none can part:
Such a Heart, as joys in love.

George Herbert, 1633